TABLE OF CONTENTS

A short note on Japanese names and the Romanization of Japanese words:

Japanese names are usually written with the surname first, followed by the given name. For the sake of simplicity and consistency, however, I have elected to adopt the Western order of writing the given name first, followed by the surname. For the Romanization of Japanese words, I have chosen to use the Revised Hepburn method.

INTRODUCTION

"Of all the people in the world, none are as unsuited to [the Christian] faith as the Japanese."[1] – Father Valente in *The Samurai*

"This country is a swamp, far more terrible than we had imagined. No matter what seedling you plant here, its roots will begin to rot. Its leaves will turn yellow and wither away. And we planted Christianity in this swamp…"[2] – Father Ferreira in *Silence*

It has become common in recent years to speak of the "explosive growth" of Christianity in Asia, and with good reason. In just one hundred years, the Christian population of Asia multiplied more than 14 times from roughly 22 million in 1900 to 313 million in 2000. In terms of the percentage of the population, it more than tripled from 2.3 percent to 8.5 percent.[3] Despite undergoing several periods of persecution, the Christian church has managed to grow significantly even in communist China, expanding from 1.5 million people in 1970 (0.2 percent) to almost 90 million by 2000 (7.1 percent).[4] Perhaps the most remarkable case has been that of South Korea, where Christians made up only 0.5 percent of the population in 1900, and today account for over 40 percent.[5]

[1] Shūsaku Endō, *Samurai*, (Tokyo: Shinchōsha, 1980; reprint 2009), 246.

[2] Shūsaku Enō, *Chinmoku [Silence]*, (Tokyo: Shinchōsha, 1966; reprint 2010), 239.

[3] David B. Barrett, George Thomas Kurian, and Todd M. Johnson, eds. *World Christian Encyclopedia: A Comparative Survey of Churches and Religions in the Modern World*, 1 (2001): 13.
[4] *Ibid.*, 191. (Saeki 1958) (Endō 1958)

And yet, just two hundred kilometers southeast of the Korean Peninsula, growth in Japan has been anemic at best, having stagnated around the 1 percent mark for decades.[6]

Why is this so? It is not due to persecution. Although Christianity was officially outlawed in Japan in 1614 and viciously persecuted for over two hundred years, the ban was lifted in 1873. Christianity has been legal now for over 140 years. By comparison, Christianity was also persecuted in Korea until freedom of religion was instituted in 1884.

Neither can the low number of Christians in Japan be explained by a lack of missionizing effort. Missionaries of all Christian denominations flocked to Japan in the mid-19th century and again following the Second World War. They have, up to this point, established over two hundred mission societies in the country.[7] Even today, one can find plenty of Christian missionaries of all denominations in all major

[5] *Ibid.*, 682.

[6] Statistics on Christianity in Japan vary quite widely across different sources. While the *World Christian Encyclopedia* gives the figure of 3.6 percent for Christians in Japan, that figure seems to include many questionable groups, such as "anonymous Christians," individuals professing an interest in Christianity but not belonging to any community, and people who call themselves Christian while simultaneously adhering to and practicing other religions. The Japanese government's census of 1990 counts only 0.7 percent. The *Kirisutokyo Nenkan Henshūbu [Christian Yearbook]* of 2002, cited by Mark R. Mullins in "Japanese Christianity," gives the figure of 0.864 percent, and the *Christian Almanac* of 2007, cited by Mase-Hasegawa, gives the figure of 0.578 percent. I have chosen to use the figure of "1 percent," as it appears to be the one most commonly cited and falls between the high figure of the *World Christian Encyclopedia* and the lower figures of the Japanese census, the *Christian Yearbook* and the *Christian Almanac*.

[7] Mark R. Mullins, "Japanese Christianity," in *Nanzan Guide to Japanese Religions*, ed. Paul L. Swanson and Clark Chilson (Honolulu, University of Hawai'i Press, 2006), 117.

Japanese cities, and yet, it seems their efforts are bearing little fruit.

So perhaps there's a lack of exposure to Christian literature? That does not seem to be the case either, as the Japan Bible Society alone sold over 20 million Bibles in the period from 1971 to 1990 – a surprisingly high figure when one considers that official statistics counted fewer than one million Christians in Japan at any one time during that same timespan. When one also considers sales of Bibles from other publishers it seems there is quite a high level of general interest among the Japanese public in Christian literature.[8]

Could the influence of Confucianism and Buddhism make Japanese less receptive to the Christian message? That does not seem to be the case either, as both China and South Korea share the same Buddhist and Confucian heritage as Japan (and, in fact, exported them to Japan), but exhibit phenomenal growth in their Christian communities.

Perhaps, one might surmise, Japan is becoming secularized like much of Europe, and its people simply have no interest in religion at all, Christian or otherwise. This explanation seems to work when one hears that only 26 percent of Japanese respondents in a recent survey described themselves as "religious."[9] It falls apart, however, when one hears that "seventy-five percent have either a Buddhist or Shinto altar in their home,"[10] half believe in "the existence of

---

[8] Yoshinobu Kumazawa, foreword to *Christianity in Japan, 1971 – 1990*, ed. Yoshinobu Kumazawa and David L. Swain, (Tokyo: Kyo Bun Kwan [The Christian Literature Society of Japan], 1991), xiii.

[9] Robert Kisala, "Japanese Religions," in *Nanzan Guide to Japanese Religions*, ed. Paul L. Swanson and Clark Chilson (Honolulu, University of Hawai'i Press, 2006), 4.

[10] Robert Kisala, "Japanese Religions," 3

gods or buddhas," two-thirds believe in an "unseen higher power," and even "one-quarter of those who described themselves as atheists [...] also professed some belief in God."[11] In fact, far from becoming more secularized, surveys suggest that younger Japanese are becoming more religious than their parents and grandparents in terms of both belief and practice.[12] In addition to all of this we see the phenomenon of the three thousand "new religions" which have cropped up in Japan since the mid-19th century and currently claim 10 to 20 percent of Japanese as members.[13] It therefore appears that Japanese people today are both open to and searching for some kind of religious or spiritual meaning in their lives.

So if the poor growth of Christianity in Japan cannot be explained by persecution, lack of evangelization efforts, the influence of Buddhism or Confucianism, the tide of secularization or any of the other aforementioned factors, is there something particular about the Japanese people that makes Christian evangelization so difficult? Is there something about Christianity that simply does not "fit" Japan? This certainly seems to be the suggestion in much of the literature of Shūsaku Endō (1923 – 1996), one of the most prominent Japanese writers of the postwar period.

Baptized as a Catholic at age 11, Endō struggled through much of his life to reconcile his 'Japaneseness' with his

---

[11] Robert Kisala, "Japanese Religions," 6.

[12] See Jan Swyngedouw, "Religion in Contemporary Japanese Society," in *Religion & Society in Modern Japan*, ed. Mark R. Mullins, Susumu Shimazono and Paul L. Swanson (Berkeley: Asian Humanities Press, 1993), 49 – 72.

[13] Susumu Shimazono, "New Religious Movements," in *Religion & Society in Modern Japan*, ed. Mark R. Mullins, Susumu Shimazono and Paul L. Swanson (Berkeley: Asian Humanities Press, 1993), 221 – 230.

Christian faith – to tailor the ill-fitting "ready-made suit" of Christianity to his Japanese body.[14] In a prolific career spanning almost fifty years, Endō published approximately 230 novels, plays, reviews and essays, many of which deal with this question of whether it is possible for a Japanese to become a true Christian.[15]

Upon an initial reading of his work, Endō appears to say that Christianity and the Japanese are like oil and water – they will never mix. Endō draws sharp distinctions between East and West, Yellow and White, Japanese and European, and makes the case that Christianity belongs solely to the West and has no place in the East (read: Japan).[16] Over and over, the Japanese people are described as being somehow different from Europeans in a way that makes them inherently incapable of accepting the Christian faith. Japan itself is described as a "mud swamp" in which it is impossible for Christianity to take root. In the words of Father Velasco, a 17th century Franciscan missionary in Endō's novel, *The Samurai*, Japan is the "*isole infortunate*" (unfortunate island) whose people will not and cannot receive the gospel.[17]

[14] Interview quoted in Emi Mase-Hasegawa, *Christ in Japanese Culture: Theological Themes in Shusaku Endo's Literary Works* (Leiden: Brill, 2008), 78.

[15] See Appendix in Mase-Hasegawa's *Christ in Japanese Culture* for a complete list of Endō's literary works.

[16] Note that Endō uses the terms "East," "Yellow," "Oriental" and "Japanese" interchangeably, and does likewise with "West," "White" and "European." The East of course consists of more than just Japan, and the West is more than just Europe. It is unclear whether, when speaking of the "East" and its "yellow" people, Endō intends to speak for all Asian peoples, or only the Japanese. For the sake of this paper, I will apply Endō's statements about "yellow people" only to the Japanese without extending them to other Asians.

[17] Endō, *Samurai*, 78.

For anyone who argues for the universal significance of the Christian gospel, this is problematic. How can the church fulfill Christ's Great Commission and "make disciples of all nations"[18] if one of these nations is not only unresponsive to the message, but incapable of responding? How can the universal Truth truly be universal if it excludes a population of 127 million out of hand? Or perhaps the bigger question is, how can the Truth truly be true if it doesn't apply to everyone?

In proclaiming the absolute incompatibility between Christianity and Japan, Endō appears to challenge the validity of the entire Christian message. Such a reading of his work, however, would ignore the deeper, more complicated interactions between what his characters say, their subconscious, their emotions, and their actions. Much like real human beings, the characters often say one thing, but do something else. They profess to believe one thing, but feel something completely different.

In this paper, I would like to argue that Endō does not truly believe that the Japanese are inherently unable to accept the Christian faith, for even as the characters in his novels – both Japanese and Western – say that Japan and Christianity are mutually exclusive, their lived experiences say otherwise. The behavior and inner voices of the characters blur the supposedly sharp lines of distinction separating "white" from "yellow," and the allegedly insurmountable chasm that separates the Japanese from the Crucified is bridged from both ends.

In this paper, I will utilize Emi Mase-Hasegawa's division of Endō's literary career into the three periods 1947-1965, 1966-1980 and 1981-1996, in order to reflect on his work.[19]

---

[18] Mt 28, 19.

In the first section of my paper, I will explore Endō's anthropology of the Japanese person as expressed in the first period of his literary career. I will focus especially on his treatment of the common and clichéd characterizations of the West as a "guilt society" as opposed to Japan as a "shame society" and the theological implications that result from these characterizations. For this section, I will use *Yellow Man* (1955), *The Sea and Poison* (1958), and to a lesser extent, *White Man* (1955). In the second section of my paper, I will address Japanese responses to Christianity as presented in the second period of Endō's career. For this section, I will use the novels *Silence* (1966) and *The Samurai* (1980). In the final section of my paper, I will look at the third period of Endō's career and illustrate how he attempts to move beyond the idea that Christianity and Japan are mutually incompatible, and towards the construction of a particularly Japanese Christian theology. For this final section of my paper, I will use Endō's final novel *Deep River* (1993). Myself being Roman Catholic, like Endō himself, I will approach Christianity from a primarily Catholic perspective.

---

[19] See Emi Mase-Hasegawa, *Christ in Japanese Culture: Theological Themes in Shusaku Endo's Literary Works*, (Leiden: Brill, 2008).

CHAPTER I: ON THE JAPANESE PERSON

§ 1. What Is The Human Person?

"What is man?"[20] This is the question posed by the Council Fathers of the Second Vatican Council in the first chapter, "The Dignity of the Human Person," of the *Pastoral Constitution on the Church in the Modern World* (*Gaudium et Spes*). The Fathers proceed to answer their own question by drawing a general outline of what the universal human being is. According to them, the human person is an "image of God" (*imago Dei*) who is "capable of knowing and loving his [*sic*] Creator."[21] Having encountered and succumbed to the temptations of evil, however, "man [*sic*] is split within himself [*sic*]," and experiences life as "a dramatic struggle between good and evil, between light and darkness."[22] Humans do not navigate the way between good and evil completely in the dark, however, as God has endowed them with a conscience. "Always summoning [human persons] to love good and avoid evil," they write, "the voice of conscience when necessary speaks to [the person's] heart: do this, shun that." They add that, "Conscience is the most secret core and sanctuary of a [person]. There he [*sic*] is alone with God, Whose voice echoes in his [*sic*] depths."[23] Humankind has freedom of the will, and

---

[20] Second Vatican Council, *Gaudium et Spes* (1965), no. 12, http://www.vatican.va/archive/hist_councils/ii_vatican_council/documents/vat-ii_cons_19651207_gaudium-et-spes_en.html [accessed May 12, 2011].

[21] *GS* 12.

[22] *GS* 13.

"for its part, authentic freedom is an exceptional sign of the divine image within [humankind]."[24] Faced with the "mystery of death," the human person instinctively "rebels against death because he [sic] bears in himself [sic] an eternal seed which cannot be reduced to sheer matter."[25] Finally, "the root reason for human dignity lies in [humankind's] call to communion with God."[26] To summarize, then, the human person is an image of God that experiences reality in dual terms (light vs. dark, good vs. evil) while being guided by an inner conscience. Furthermore, the human person has free will, resists death, and is destined for communion with God. There is of course far more to this chapter, but these are the characterizations most relevant to a discussion of Endō's work.

In a commentary on Endō's novel, *The Sea and Poison*, literary critic Shōichi Saeki writes, "The question that never leaves Shūsaku Endō's mind is this: 'What kind of human being is the Japanese person'?"[27] Indeed this question dominates the pages not only of *The Sea and Poison*, but of Endō's earlier novella *Yellow Man* as well. The portrait of the Japanese person that emerges from these works is remarkably different from the Second Vatican Council's description of the universal human being, especially in areas concerning conscience, guilt, consciousness of sin, freedom of the will and attitudes to death. The Japanese person, as portrayed in these

---

[23] *GS* 16.

[24] *GS* 17.

[25] *GS* 18.

[26] *GS* 19.

[27] Shōichi Saeki, commentary to *Umi to Dokuyaku* [*The Sea and Poison*] by Shūsaku Endō (Tokyo: Shinchōsha, 1958; reprint 2010), 197.

works, does not experience life as a dramatic struggle between good and evil, does not in fact recognize evil when he or she sees it, has no conscience, has no real freedom of choice and is indifferent to death.

§ 2. THE JAPANESE PERSON IN *YELLOW MAN*

Yellow Man takes place in Japan towards the end of the Second World War. It starts out in the form of a letter from the young Japanese man Minoru Chiba to the French priest Father Brou, who is being detained in the Takatsuki concentration camp. Chiba is writing to inform Father Brou that the other missionary in the community, Pierre Durand, has died. He encloses Durand's diary in the letter, and the rest of the novella alternates between sections of Chiba's letter to Father Brou and excerpts from Durand's diary.

As the story unfolds, the reader learns that Chiba is a baptized Catholic, but he no longer practices his faith. For the last two years, he has been having a sexual affair with his cousin Itoko, who also happens to be his best friend's fiancée. Durand was formerly a priest, but was disgraced and ostracized from the community after beginning a sexual affair with the Japanese woman Kimiko. Father Brou is the only one who still treats Durand with any respect, and has been financially supporting the destitute Durand and Kimiko for the last eight years. Despite Father Brou's continual kindness, Durand betrays him by planting a gun in his office and informing the Kempeitai – the Imperial Japanese Army's notoriously brutal military police – of the hidden weapon. This leads to Father Brou's arrest and internment in a concentration camp. Chiba confesses to Father Brou that he knew of the gun and could have warned the priest, but failed to do so out of an overwhelming sense of paralyzing fatigue.

The two "writers" of the novella, Chiba and Durand, have much in common. Both have committed sexual crimes with partners who would usually be considered off-limits, and both betray Father Brou – Durand by planting the gun and Chiba by failing to warn him. Both men are neck-deep in sin. Their responses to their sin, however, are radically different. While Durand is consumed with guilt and terror of his impending judgment at the hand of God, Chiba is almost entirely indifferent to his own fate. Endō ascribes these differences not to any personal characteristics of the two men, but to their respective races.

In the first section of his letter to Father Brou, Chiba confesses that he has never truly understood what sin is, not even when he went to confession as a child. He adds, "A yellow person like me doesn't have these serious, exaggerated things like consciousness of sin and nihilism. Not like you [white people]. I don't have any of that in me at all. All I have is fatigue – this deep fatigue."[28] Even when he begins sleeping with his cousin, thereby betraying his friend Saeki, he feels nothing but the heavy inertia of this tiredness. "I kept on violating Itoko after [the first time]," he writes, "loading more of that deep fatigue onto my constricted back. I felt neither the agony of sin nor the pangs of conscience. I felt a little sorry for Saeki, but there's nothing I can do. I feel like I'm just rolling down a dark slope."[29] In this way, Endō introduces two aspects of Chiba's character – the lack of any consciousness of sin and this deep, paralyzing sense of fatigue. The two are

[28] Shūsaku Endō, *Shiroi Hito Kiiroi Hito [White Man, Yellow Man]*, (Tokyo: Shinchōsha, 1955; reprint 2010), 91.

[29] Endō, *White Man, Yellow Man*, 98.

completely bound up with each other and lead further to apathy and a fatalistic attitude towards everything.

This fatigue remains with Chiba throughout the story, dominating his character and paralyzing him from any action. He stops attending Mass, not out of any existential crisis of faith, but simply out of fatigue.[30] Even when confronted with the possibility of saving another human being's life, the fatigue prevents him from taking any action. While working at his uncle's hospital, he notices a problem with a tuberculosis patient's pulse. Though all he has to do is press a button to call for a nurse or doctor, the fatigue weighs down his arm, and he does nothing, with the result that the patient dies.[31]

A general numbness permeates Chiba, growing stronger as he continues to sleep with his best friend's fiancée while at the same time nearing death from tuberculosis. He has lost all interest in the outcome of the war, the fates of his friends who are fighting in the Pacific, and even in his own death.[32] Several times, he mentions the inevitability of death at the hands of the approaching American B29 bombers and the futility of doing anything to prevent death. Even after being shot at by a low-flying American fighter plane, all he can say is, "Death is just a natural part of life. Only the movement of [the fighter plane] and the vibrations of the machine disturbed the sweetness of death."[33] Though he has been brought up as a Christian, this fatalism and resignation towards death feature far more powerfully within him than the Christianity he has

---

[30] Endō, *White Man, Yellow Man*, 93.

[31] Endō, *White Man, Yellow Man*, 142.

[32] Endō, *White Man, Yellow Man*, 94.

[33] Endō, *White Man, Yellow Man*, 131.

learned from the missionaries. "I will keep sleeping with Itoko, deteriorate and die, and there's nothing else I can do," he writes. "This dark resignation that I feel is stronger than the Christian logic you [Father Brou] taught me."[34]

There is of course the possibility that Chiba's fatalism, indifference towards sin, lack of consciousness and resignation to death are the result not of his being "yellow," but of his deteriorating health and the external circumstances of the war. Chiba himself wonders whether this could be the case.[35] Significantly, however, the other Japanese characters Itoko and Kimiko also seem to suffer from the same afflictions as Chiba, while the Westerner Durand does not – he seems to suffer from precisely the opposite problems. Furthermore, Durand's descriptions of Japanese people confirm the notion that the numbness towards sin, lack of conscience and indifference towards death are inherent to the Japanese ethos and not simply a byproduct of the extraordinary circumstances of the war.

As opposed to Chiba, who feels neither guilt nor sin, Durand is tormented by guilt at having betrayed the church by breaking his vow of chastity, and he is absolutely consumed, perhaps even obsessed, by his fear of death and damnation. In his first diary entry, he describes how he closed his eyes and saw his own face at the time of death. "That was the look of someone going to Hell," he writes. "It was the face of Judas who betrayed Christ and hung himself."[36] Thinking about his impending doom and the eternity of torment awaiting him, he screams in despair.[37] He looks with envy to

[34] Endō, *White Man, Yellow Man*, 99.

[35] Endō, *White Man, Yellow Man*, 130

[36] Endō, *White Man, Yellow Man*, 105, 106.

his Japanese wife Kimiko who is indifferent to God, sin, and conscience, and therefore free of the agonizing guilt and fear of death that torment him. She asks him why he doesn't simply forget about God and turn to the all-forgiving Buddha, thereby relieving himself of his fear and agony. This comes as a revelation to Durand. Finally, twelve years after coming to Japan to missionize, he has understood the good fortune of the pagans. He has discovered "the secret in the eyes of Kimiko and that young man Chiba. Those thin, muddy eyes characteristic of the yellow people [...] numb to God and sin, indifferent to death."[38] He thinks that he has found salvation via the road of the pagans, so diametrically opposed to the "white" ideas with which he has grown up.

Having discovered the path to salvation, Durand resolves to become like Kimiko and Chiba by forgetting God and piling sin upon sin until he becomes numb to both sin and death. This impels him to his second act of betrayal, namely, planting the gun in his benefactor Father Brou's office. After planting the gun, but before tipping off the police, Durand has one last conversation with Father Brou. The latter believes in the universality of the Catholic faith, but the now "converted" Durand disagrees, saying, "Think of the average Japanese person. Do you think he needs the Lord God? Do you think he can truly experience Christ?"[39] Durand is convinced that Brou has not seen the eyes of yellow people like Kimiko and Chiba, whereas he has discovered their secret.

Unfortunately for Durand, his sense of salvation is premature, for as soon as he leaves Father Brou, he sees his

[37] Endō, *White Man, Yellow Man*, 133.

[38] Endō, *White Man, Yellow Man*, 136.

[39] Endō, *White Man, Yellow Man*, 152.

death face again. This time, the face is already in Hell. He realizes at this moment that, being a white man, he can neither reject God nor deny God's existence. God permeates every fiber of his being, down to the "tips of [his] fingers." He looks at his hands and sees the palms of "a race that must choose between believing in or resenting God." All the Japanese people around him, however, including Kimiko and Chiba, "can do everything without God. They're numb and indifferent to the church, the agony of sin, the hope for salvation, all the things we white people had thought were conditions for being human. They just live in perpetual ambiguity. How is this possible? How is this possible?"[40]

Through the characters in *Yellow Man*, Endō describes a series of supposedly fundamental differences between white and yellow people. To summarize, yellow people have no sense of sin, no conscience, no guilt, and no idea of God. They just experience a perpetual fatigue, a deep fatalism, and an indifference towards death. White people, on the other hand, have an acute sense of sin, conscience, and guilt. They can resent God, but they can never shut God out of their lives. Far from being indifferent to death, they are consumed by the specter of eternal damnation in Hell.

Once this dichotomy is established, one can see why Endō quotes the Apocalypse of St. John (or Book of Revelation) in the preface to *Yellow Man* and what relevance this has to the Japanese person's relationship to the Divine. "I know your works; you are neither cold nor hot. I wish that you were either cold or hot. So, because you are lukewarm, and neither cold nor hot, I am about to spit you out of my mouth."[11] Durand, the white man, is clearly hot with guilt,

---

[40] Endō, *White Man, Yellow Man*, 154.

resentment, fear, and possibly even hatred. Chiba, Itoko and Kimiko, however, are tepid. They don't care about anything and simply wander through life as if they're half-asleep. If this is a part of what it means to be yellow or Japanese, are all Japanese destined to be "spat out"?

Endō continues his exploration of the Japanese person and its relationship to sin, evil and guilt in *The Sea and Poison*, published three years after *Yellow Man*.

§ 3. THE JAPANESE PERSON IN *THE SEA AND POISON*

Like *Yellow Man*, *The Sea and Poison* takes place in Japan towards the end of the Second World War. It is based on the true story of a series of vivisections performed on American prisoners of war in a university hospital. Endō creates a fictionalized version of the grisly story in an attempt to figure out how and why these doctors, nurses, and medical students – all seemingly normal people – could commit such an abhorrent crime. As with *Yellow Man*, readers are presented with a disturbing view of the Japanese person, perhaps best encapsulated by Endō's use of the term *bukimi*, meaning "weird" or "creepy" in the sense of sending shivers down one's spine and stimulating an almost instinctive sense of repulsion. Whereas *Yellow Man* focuses on Japanese insensitivities to sin, conscience and guilt, *The Sea and Poison* investigates the common yet controversial characterization of Japan as a "shame culture" as opposed to the West's "guilt culture."

Before turning to the novel itself, it is perhaps important to note that Endō was not the first person to portray Japan as a "shame culture." The idea comes from the American Ruth Benedict's landmark ethnography of Japan, *The*

---

[41] Ap 3,15-16, quoted on p. 88 of *White Man, Yellow Man*.

Chrysanthemum and the Sword: Patterns of Japanese Culture, published in 1946. Benedict's work, of which a widely-read Japanese translation was published in 1948, has undeniably been extremely influential in the field of Japanese studies. It has also been highly controversial for its assessments of Japanese people and their cultures, especially concerning the aforementioned description of Japan as a "shame culture."

According to Benedict, a guilt culture is by definition "a society that inculcates absolute standards of morality and relies on men's [sic] developing a conscience."[42] When someone transgresses these absolute standards of morality, he or she will feel bad about it regardless of whether or not anyone else discovers the crime. It is the internalized conscience that tells the person that he or she has committed a sin, and this brings about the feeling of guilt. The feelings of guilt are only relieved when the person confesses his or her transgression. Morality, guilt and conscience are all bound up with each other, so people will hopefully do what is right out of a personal and internal desire to avoid what is wrong. Benedict proposes the United States as an example of a "guilt culture," especially in its Puritan origins of the 17th century.

Japan, on the other hand, is a "shame culture." Benedict writes that "true shame cultures rely on external sanctions for good behavior, not, as true guilt cultures do, on an internalized conviction of sin. Shame is a reaction to other people's criticism," and, "So long as [someone's] bad behavior does not 'get out into the world' he need not be troubled."[43] In other words, someone brought up in a shame culture would

---

[42] Ruth Benedict, *The Chrysanthemum and the Sword: Patterns of Japanese Culture*, New edition ed., (London: Routledge & Kegan Paul Limited, 1977), 156.

[43] Ruth Benedict, 156, 157.

not feel bad about any crimes he or she has committed as long as nobody else found out about them or criticized them. Such a system of morality of course invites a few difficulties. If a crime were guaranteed never to be uncovered, would there no longer be any deterrent against committing it? If some act that Westerners would consider to be "intrinsically evil" were to be tolerated or even encouraged by one's peers instead of being criticized, would people have no qualms about doing them? Would people brought up in a shame culture never develop a conscience? And what would a culture with no absolute standards of morality look like?

These questions feature prominently in *The Sea and Poison*. The book mainly centers on the character of Suguro, a medical student at the university hospital in Fukuoka, but Endō also devotes a considerable number of pages to the investigation of Suguro's friend Toda – another medical student – and the nurse Ueda. It is in the treatment of Toda that the problem of the shame culture comes to the fore.

Suguro, who is the main protagonist of the novel, is young, naïve, and to a large extent, rather innocent. Having grown up in the countryside, he does not understand and cannot keep up with all the political wheeling and dealing that goes on behind the scenes at the medical school. The streetwise and cynical Toda, on the other hand, understands exactly what's going on as professors compete for higher positions within the university's hierarchy, using patients as pawns in their power games. Whereas Suguro often allows his emotions and feelings of compassion for his patients to dictate his actions, Toda knows better. He fancies himself as someone who is absolutely rational and objective. He is a "realist."

In a section of the book called "Those Who Will Be Judged," Toda testifies in the first person, describing how he came to be the person he is. Internally, that is to say, within the text, the audience appears to be a jury at his trial, but this audience can be extended externally to break the fourth wall so that Endō is addressing the general readership of the novel, or perhaps the Japanese people, through Toda's testimony.

Toda digs deep into his own past, beginning with an account of his experiences in elementary school. He explains how he learned from an early age that receiving praise from his teachers was not so much dependent on actually being good, but on saying and doing the right things at the right times. Whether his actions were motivated out of a genuine desire to do good or simply out of a desire to look good was inconsequential, as the teachers only saw the external side anyway. He describes how he once witnessed a classmate being bullied. At first he did nothing to help, as he also harbored a dislike for the child. Once he noticed a teacher approaching, however, he heroically rushed to his classmate's aid, stopped the fight and reprimanded the bullies, all the while pretending that he had never noticed the teacher approaching. The teacher praised him as a shining example of virtue.[44] Before allowing his audience to criticize him as "sly," "dishonest" or "an opportunist," Toda challenges his audience to examine themselves. "Even as I write this, I don't look back upon my past self and think I was a particularly dishonest boy. I want you to look back on your own childhoods. Any child with even a modicum of intelligence has this degree of sneakiness, and at some point, they're deluded into believing this makes them 'good'."[45] Interesting to note here is his usage of the term "deluded" (sakkaku). As people grow up, they

[44] Shūsaku Endō, Umi to Dokuyaku [The Sea and Poison], (Tokyo: Shinchōsha, 1958; reprint 2010), 127.

[45] Endō, The Sea and Poison, 121.

actually come to believe that they're doing and being good, even when they are not. Toda's audience, and by extension the reader of the novel, is invited to ask him or herself whether he or she is truly a good person or if he or she has simply learned to "game the system" like he has.

Toda was not deluded. Even as a child, he recognized that the motivations underlying actions are important, and acknowledged that his own actions were not truly good because he was always motivated by some reward. Seeking escape from the gnawing sense of dissatisfaction with himself, he took his most prized possession, a fountain pen his father brought to him from Germany, and gave it to a classmate, sternly telling his classmate not to tell anyone. Here was an act of true giving – giving without seeking reward. But this act of true goodness brought him no relief. "I felt a pale void in my heart," he says. "I felt not a single drop of this so-called 'good conscience' or satisfaction at having done something good..."[46]

Toda goes on to recount several more anecdotes from his adolescence and youth. He describes an incident from his high school days, in which he stole and destroyed his teacher's prize specimen of a rare butterfly. Another student was accused of and punished for the crime. At first, Toda felt terrible, especially because the falsely accused classmate accepted the punishment without trying to defend his innocence. He found it hard to breathe, dreamt about the boy, and even got a toothache out of guilt. That all evaporated instantaneously, however, when he saw the boy boasting about having committed the crime, thereby winning admiration from the other classmates.[47]

---

[46] Endō, *The Sea and Poison*, 131.

[47] Endō, *The Sea and Poison*, 134-136.

From these and other experiences peppered throughout his childhood and adolescence, Toda learned something about his so-called "conscience," saying, "Already from the time I was a child, these so-called 'pangs of conscience' were nothing but the fear of society's punishments and other people's perceptions of me."[48] He describes further "sins" he committed as an adult, such as adultery. He slept with his married cousin and initially felt bad about it, but felt fine once he was assured that nobody would find out, and got on with his life as a medical student.[49] At this point, he makes a further confession. He writes that he not only feels no guilt for any crimes he has committed, he also feels absolutely no compassion when he sees others suffering. As a medical student, he sees patients suffering and dying, sometimes at his own hands, but he doesn't care. Their loved ones and relatives cry, but he feels nothing. On a more personal level, he recounts how he slept with his housemaid, got her pregnant, performed a dangerous home abortion, and then abandoned her, but far from feeling any guilt, he didn't and doesn't care.[50] Though he acknowledges that all of his crimes are despicable, he feels no pangs of conscience, not even as he is writing his testimony. "So why did I write this account today?" he asks. "Because it's *bukimi* (disturbing). I'm beginning to feel disturbed by myself – this person who fears nothing but society's punishments and the perceptions of others. And when those are removed, all that fear disappears. I am *bukimi*."[51]

---

[48] Endō, *The Sea and Poison*, 137.

[49] Endō, *The Sea and Poison*, 137-147.

[50] Endō, *The Sea and Poison*, 142, 143.

One could suppose at this point that Toda is a sociopath and a complete aberration from the norm. He sounds so callous and inhuman that there's no way his behavior and sentiments could be applied to any larger group. But it is also here that he turns to his audience once again and challenges them to look at themselves.

> Maybe *bukimi* is a bit of an exaggeration. "Strange" might be more appropriate. I want to ask you, if you peel away just one layer of skin, would you also be indifferent to the death and suffering of others like I am? Whenever you've committed some minor acts of evil and escaped punishment from society, have you also carried on without feeling much guilt or shame? And have you ever looked at yourself behaving like this and been mystified?[52]

For Toda, external sanctions, and not his own conscience, determine the internal, emotional reactions to any of his actions. As long as nobody punishes him or thinks of him negatively, he doesn't care. Societal responses not only dictate his internal reactions towards his actions, they also motivate or deter him from the actions in the first place. If he expects a reward, he will do something good, and if he expects to be caught and punished, he will avoid doing bad. If he expects no punishment, there's nothing to stop him from doing the bad. He fits perfectly into the "shame culture" as defined by Ruth Benedict.

Almost as if to drive home the point that Toda is no exceptional anomaly, Endō has Toda end his testimony with

---

[51] Endō, *The Sea and Poison*, 144.

[52] Endō, *The Sea and Poison*, 144.

an observation about two of the other participants in the vivisection of the American soldier.

> The day before yesterday, when Assistant Professor Shibata and Doctor Asai told us about 'the act,' I looked into the bluish-white flames in the brazier and asked myself, after I do this, will I be plagued by a bad conscience? Will I shudder at the murder I've committed? Killing a live human being… will I suffer for the rest of my life after doing something so monstrous? I looked up. Assistant Professor Shibata and Doctor Asai even had smiles on their faces. They're just like me after all. Even if we are punished one day, their fear is only directed towards the punishment they'll receive from society, and not their own consciences.[53]

Endō returns to using third-person narrative to describe the actual vivisection and Toda mostly fades into the background, but he and his questions reappear in the description of the procedure's immediate aftermath. Endō writes, "What Toda wanted more than anything now was torment. An intense pain in his chest. A heart-rending feeling of regret. But even when he went back to the operating room, no such feelings emerged."[54] Toda asks himself, "Do I have no conscience? Not just me, but the others as well. Are we all numb to the crimes we commit?"[55]

One often hears of soldiers having to dehumanize the enemy in order to be able to kill without feeling too much remorse or guilt. One also hears about veterans trying to block

---

[53] Endō, *The Sea and Poison*, 146, 147.

[54] Endō, *The Sea and Poison*, 181, 182.

[55] Endō, *The Sea and Poison*, 182.

incidents from their memories and refusing to ever talk about them again, as doing so is too painful and taxing on their consciences. For Toda, the problem is entirely reversed. He seeks remorse, but cannot find it, even when he actively returns to the scene of the crime.

It is significant that, at this point, Endō spends much time discussing Toda's upbringing in Japan's "shame culture," and also that Toda turns directly to the readership several times and asks them to examine themselves. Both Toda and his crimes are, of course, exceptional cases, but the questions Endō raises are broad. What happens to people who grow up in the "shame culture" of Japan? Do they ever make ethical or moral decisions out of internal motivations rather than solely external ones of reward and punishment? And if actions are based solely on external sanctions and rewards, what does that say about their humanity? Do such people have the capacity for compassion? Do they have a conscience? If not, are they even capable of having or developing a conscience?

There is, of course, more to *The Sea and Poison* than just these questions, and Endō explores the human capacity for evil through many other motivators such as ambition, fear, coercion, anger and pain. Many of these other motivators are, one assumes, universally human. The effects of growing up in a "shame culture" would, however, seem to be more particular to the Japanese, and it is here that one can find Endō's attempts at answering the question, "What kind of human being is the Japanese person?" In one word, Endō's answer seems to be, "*bukimi*."

§ 4. CAN THE JAPANESE PERSON BE CONSIDERED AN IMAGO DEI?

So far, Endō's description of the Japanese person does not yield a very flattering or hopeful picture. As stated above, the Japanese person in *Yellow Man* has no concept of sin, conscience, guilt, or God. He or she simply experiences a perpetual fatigue, a deep fatalism, and an indifference towards death. *The Sea and Poison* reinforces the notion that Japanese people have no conscience or guilt, and surmises that this is the result of growing up in a "shame culture." As portrayed through the character of Toda, it seems the Japanese are incapable of having a conscience, even if they want one. In addition to these characterizations, several of the themes apparent in *Yellow Man* appear again in *The Sea and Poison*, such as the paralyzing fatigue, the fatalism and the ignorance of God.

If these descriptions are indeed accurate in their portrayal of the Japanese person, the Roman Catholic Church has a problem, for these characterizations stand quite at odds with the description of the human person as developed in *Gaudium et Spes*. As stated above, the Council Fathers make several assertions about the nature of the human being. The question is whether they are really applicable to people from all over the world. The characters in Endō's *Yellow Man* and *The Sea and Poison* would seem to say, "No," for it seems that, although they apply to people from the West, they do not apply to the Japanese. And if it doesn't apply to the Japanese, how many other people groups could be similarly excluded?

Regarding humans' internal battles between good and evil, the Council Fathers say that, "man [*sic*] is split within himself. As a result, all of human life, whether individual or collective, shows itself to be a dramatic struggle between good and evil, between light and darkness."[56] Although *Yellow Man*

56 Second Vatican Council, *Gaudium et Spes* (1965), no. 13,

was published ten years before the promulgation of *Gaudium et Spes*, the character of Chiba seems to contradict this statement directly. He opens his letter by stating, "White people like you and Durand can create tragedy and comedy in your lives, but no drama exists in me."[57] He then closes his letter to Father Brou with, "It's midnight already. I had forgotten it was Christmas Eve. For you, this must be the night when God brought light into this darkness. But for yellow people like me, there is no distinction between light and darkness."[58] The Council Fathers speak of drama and the dualistic conflicts between good and evil being common to the human condition. Chiba says that while these things may apply to white people, they do not apply to Japanese.

Regarding conscience, the Council Fathers write that, "In the depths of his conscience, man [*sic*] detects a law which he [*sic*] does not impose upon himself [*sic*], but which holds him [*sic*] to obedience. Always summoning him [*sic*] to love good and avoid evil, the voice of conscience when necessary speaks to his [*sic*] heart: do this, shun that," and so on.[59] Toda would clearly protest at this point, insisting that he has no conscience and could not awaken one, even when he tried. There is nothing guiding him but his fear of punishment and desire for reward. Having or not having a conscience would seem to depend on upbringing, and, for Toda, on being brought up in a "guilt culture" instead of a "shame culture."

http://www.vatican.va/archive/hist_councils/ii_vatican_council/docum ents/vat-ii_cons_19651207_gaudium-et-spes_en.html [accessed May 12, 2011].

[57] Endō, *White Man, Yellow Man*, 90.

[58] Endō, *White Man, Yellow Man*, 161.

[59] *GS* 16.

The conciliar document goes on to talk about human freedom, saying that, "Only in freedom can man [sic] direct himself [sic] toward goodness. [...] For its part, authentic freedom is an exceptional sign of the divine image within man [sic]. For God has willed that man [sic] remain 'under the control of his [sic] own decisions.'"[60] Here, both Chiba and Suguro would protest. The fatalistic Chiba would point to the immense fatigue that paralyzes him from taking any action whatsoever and his own inevitable death through American bombing raids over which he has no control. Though not discussed above, Suguro would refer to his sense of weakness, the pressure exerted on him to participate in the vivisection by his superiors,[61] and his complete lack of control over his own fate as represented in a dream in which he was being swept away like a small woodchip on the dark sea.[62]

Finally, there is the issue of humankind's reaction to death. The Council Fathers write that,

> It is in the face of death that the riddle a [sic] human existence grows most acute. Not only is man tormented by pain and by the advancing deterioration of his body, but

[60] GS 17.

[61] When first asked to participate in the vivisection, Suguro is told that he's free to decide whether or not he'll participate. The way in which Dr. Asai asks him, however, indicates subtle but heavy pressure. "'So, what'll it be, Suguro?' asked Dr. Asai, bringing his face closer to Suguro's and catching the light in his frameless glasses. 'You're free to choose. Really.'" (p. 88) There is also quite clearly some pressure from above, as the leaders of Suguro's department are staking their hopes for promotion on their collaboration with the military's experimentation. They need a full team of doctors, interns and nurses for the procedure, so if Suguro declines, he lets down both his superiors and the prestige of the entire department. Suguro is clearly pressured, some would say he was coerced.

[62] Endō, *The Sea and Poison*, 88.

even more so by a dread of perpetual extinction. He rightly follows the intuition of his heart when he abhors and repudiates the utter ruin and total disappearance of his own person. He rebels against death because he bears in himself an eternal seed which cannot be reduced to sheer matter.[63]

Durand in *Yellow Man* clearly seems to fit this description, although he seems to fear damnation more than extinction. Chiba, on the other hand, doesn't seem to care, and neither do Kimiko, Itoko and Toda.

Based on what Endō's characters reveal about themselves in *Yellow Man* and *The Sea and Poison*, it seems that the Council Fathers' assumptions about the human being are not at all universal, but very much confined to the West. When it comes to the oriental person, and specifically the Japanese, the Second Vatican Council's image of the human person simply doesn't fit Endō's characterization.

Given the incongruities between the Second Vatican Council's image of the human person and the radically different image of the Japanese person as portrayed in Endō's characters, can a Japanese still be considered an *imago Dei*? The character Durand certainly seems to think not. Looking at his wife Kimiko, he says, "No face was as far removed from God as the face of this oriental woman."[64] It appears that Father Valente's comment in *The Samurai*, that "of all the people in the world, none are as unsuited to [the Christian] faith as the Japanese,"[65] is accurate, and they will indeed be "spat out" by God.

---

[63] *GS* 18.

[64] Endō, *White Man, Yellow Man*, 119

§ 5. A More Nuanced View of the Japanese Person

There is, however, another level to Endō's work, namely, that of the lived experiences of his characters. While his characters say many things about themselves and each other, oftentimes their actions, emotions and reactions contradict their own words. When one looks beyond the words the characters speak and looks instead at what they do and feel, the supposedly stark differences between white and yellow begin to blur.

First, there is the question of whether or not Japanese can recognize sin. Chiba repeatedly says he cannot, and Durand also says Japanese have no concept of it. On a *subconscious* level, however, Chiba *does* appear to recognize sin. He visits Durand's house and smells a "nauseating odor" he's never smelled before. He smells it wafting from Durand's mouth as the latter tries to lie to him and tell him that the pistol belongs to Father Brou. When Chiba leaves the house, he gulps down fresh air in order to cleanse himself of that awful odor. In his letter to Father Brou, he writes that, "the nauseating odor in Durand's house was definitely not the smell of a rotting old house. I think that if sin had a smell... if hatred, envy and curses could have an odor, that would be it."[66] Chiba notices the odor again later in the story when Durand tries to threaten Chiba not to incriminate him.[67] It seems that Chiba, even as he says he does not understand sin, does have some kind of intuitive aversion to it. While he himself is committing sin by

---

[65] Endō, *Samurai*, 246.

[66] Endō, *White Man, Yellow Man*, 128.

[67] Endō, *White Man, Yellow Man*, 143.

sleeping with his friend's fiancée, he does not notice it, but he does recognize it in others.

Nevertheless, the moment does eventually come when Chiba recognizes his own sin. Chiba's friend and Itoko's fiancée, Saeki, has joined a Kamikaze special attack unit. He is returning home on Christmas Eve for one last night with Itoko before he ships out for his suicide mission. Itoko tells Chiba she doesn't want to sleep with him just for this one night, but Chiba ignores her pleas and lies with her anyway. He drops her off at the station, and as he passes the church on his walk home, he feels something:

> Saeki is coming back on Christmas Eve. He's spending one last day with Itoko in this village, then going to Kyūshū to board a kamikaze plane. I knew all that, and I slept with Itoko anyway. Father [Brou], at this moment, for the first time, I felt a slight pain in my chest. It wasn't anything intense like the pangs of conscience or fear of sin. It was something I suppose to be essentially different from those. The pain was faint, as if I'd been pricked in the chest by the point of a single needle.[68]

The pain is only slight, and Chiba is quick to dismiss it as not being the realization of his own sin. However, the mere fact that he rushes to negate the significance of this sensation seems to suggest that perhaps his eyes have been opened.

The pain moves Chiba to action, and for the first time in two months, he resolves to do something. It appears that the "voice of conscience" has "spoken to his heart."[69] He goes into the church to warn Father Brou about the gun Durand has

---

[68] Endō, *White Man, Yellow Man*, 146.

[69] *GS*, 16.

planted, but unfortunately, Father Brou is not there at the moment. The next chance he has to warn Father Brou, Chiba once again succumbs to his fatigue and does nothing. It is on that day that Father Brou is arrested.

Though the stimulus to act was short-lived and ultimately did not accomplish anything, the fact that Chiba did at least try to warn Father Brou is significant. Something did move him to do good, even if the motivation wasn't strong enough to actually make him do it in the end. Chiba reflects on his actions, his inactions, and their effects on those around him:

> When I think about it, I had returned to Nigawa simply because I didn't want to move anymore. Nevertheless, in the span of just two months, the lives of several people have been changed for my sake like rocks get wet and change shape as water flows over them. Saeki was one of these people. The youth who died in the hospital three days ago was another. He probably would have died anyway, but if I had called the nurse, he may have been given a dose of camphor, and he might have lived another half hour. You [Father Brou] may eventually have been arrested by the police anyway, but if I had told you about Durand's gun, you would probably not have been sent to Takatsuki [concentration camp] by the military police. I thought about my karma. Even if people do nothing but lie in bed all day like tuberculosis patients, they still create ripples around them. That is a strange and mysterious fact. But how can I, at this point, remove this heavy weight from myself?[70]

Chiba's eyes are opened, and he realizes how everything he does affects somebody, even if he does nothing at all. He sees

---

[70] Endō, *White Man, Yellow Man*, 146, 147.

that all people are connected to each other. His sins are not inconsequential. Unfortunately, his revelation does not change his actions. The "weight" is still too heavy for him to shake. Nevertheless, there does appear to be a glimpse of something resembling a conscience within him. He is not entirely numb to conscience and sin, as Durand and even Chiba himself insist.

The Sea and Poison's Toda, on the other hand, never seems to feel or hear his conscience. At one point, all his crimes come streaming back into his memory, and he becomes convinced that he will one day be punished, but unlike with Chiba, no feelings of distress accompany this realization, and he is not motivated to change any of his actions.[71] From beginning to end, he remains cold and uncaring, despite his own abhorrence of himself and his futile search for the torment of guilt.[72]

Although Toda doesn't appear to have much of a human side, his fellow medical intern Suguro, who is arguably the main protagonist of *The Sea and Poison*, does. He shares some "yellow" characteristics with Chiba, such as his fatalism and a perpetual sense of fatigue. He is also too weak to say no to his superiors when they ask him to participate in the vivisection. Nevertheless, an internal voice within him does "speak to his heart," protesting against both the evil surrounding him and his own complicity in it.

The climax of the novel comes in the vivisection of the American prisoner of war. Suguro's job is to check the degree

---

[71] Endō, *The Sea and Poison*, 145, 146.

[72] Of course, there is also the possibility that Toda's desire to feel guilt is indicative of his search for his own humanity. Even if he is ultimately unsuccessful in feeling anything, the mere fact that he is disturbed by himself and goes in search of his conscience says something.

to which the ether has penetrated the subject. The surgeons, interns and nurses begin preparing for the experiment, and it is only then that Suguro realizes the gravity of what they are about to do. The voice inside him says, "We're going to murder a human being!"[73] By contrast, Toda cannot grasp this fact, and from beginning to end, it just feels like a normal medical procedure to him.[74] The narrator writes that when Suguro comes to his terrible realization, "Anxiety and fear suddenly began to spread throughout his chest like a black cloud." He grabs the doorknob and is about to run away, but the "thick wall" of military officers on the other side of the door intimidate him, and he is unable to escape.[75] He remains in the operating room and the experiment begins, but he refuses to carry out his duties.[76] At one point, he feels a strong urge to shove all the military officers out of the way, grab the costotome (rib-cutting tool) from Dr. Hashimoto and stop the experiment, but he is once again intimidated by the officers.[77] The voice inside him has spoken, albeit a bit too late. It is not powerful enough to make him leave the room completely or stand up to the others, but it does end his direct participation in the crime.

When the experiment is over, Suguro continues hearing the voice speaking to him. This time, he enters into conversation with it.

---

[73] Endō, *The Sea and Poison*, 152.

[74] Endō, *The Sea and Poison*, 163.

[75] Endō, *The Sea and Poison*, 152.

[76] Endō, *The Sea and Poison*, 157.

[77] Endō, *The Sea and Poison*, 170.

We killed him, we killed him, we killed him... someone's voice repeated rhythmically into his ear. (I didn't do anything.) Suguro tried his best to silence the voice. (I didn't do anything.) But this excuse ricocheted off his heart, spun around in a small spiral and disappeared. (Yes, that's true. You did nothing, [...] but you were there. You were there, and yet you did nothing.)[78]

Suguro's proclamation of innocence is turned into an accusation. The "I did nothing bad" becomes a "You did nothing to stop the bad."

One might suppose at this point that Suguro is perhaps only gripped by an intense fear of punishment and not troubled by any sense of guilt at having committed an objectively evil act. At least in the immediate future, however, he expects no punishment. What he expects is simply for things to go on as normal. It is not the prospect of any punishment that troubles him, but the very act of having killed another human being.

From tomorrow, my life as a researcher will begin again. Professor Hashimoto, Assistant Professor Shibata, Dr. Asai, Toda and all the others will go back to doing the hospital rounds and attending to patients as always. Can they really do that? That prisoner with the chestnut-colored hair seemed like a decent man. Will his face vanish completely from their minds? I can't do it. I cannot forget.[79]

The internal voice returns once again and says, "You have utterly ruined your life."[80]

---

[78] Endō, *The Sea and Poison*, 173.

[79] Endō, *The Sea and Poison*, 174.

Suguro clearly feels the guilt. He experiences the "pangs of conscience" that Toda had sought but never found. For Endō, the most *bukimi* thing about the Japanese people in his stories is that they react with indifference to evil and the crimes they commit. The most terrifying thing is not the realization that they are capable of committing evil but that, after committing evil, they can carry on with their lives as if nothing had happened.

This is made especially clear in the opening chapter of *The Sea and Poison*. Endō describes two regular Japanese men in postwar Japan. Both are veterans of the war in China. One, the owner of a petrol station, cheerfully recounts how much fun he had in China, "doing" as many women as he wanted and tying men to trees for use as bayonet practice. The other man now owns a clothing boutique, but was a member of the notoriously brutal Kempeitai military police during the war. He apparently "ran amok" in Nanking – an allusion to the Nanking Massacre in which, according to the Tokyo war crimes trials, 200,000 civilians were killed and tens of thousands of women were raped over the course of six weeks. Now that the war is over, both men live completely normal lives, seemingly unaffected by their own crimes.[81] How can one see the *imago Dei* in such people?

In the character of Suguro, and to some extent even in Chiba, Endō protests that not all Japanese are like this. Suguro was brought up in the same "shame culture" as Toda and the others, but unlike Toda, he is not solely motivated by external rewards and sanctions. He reacts instinctively to the sight of seeing another human person being murdered, even if this

---

[80] Endō, *The Sea and Poison*, 175.

[81] Endō, *The Sea and Poison*, 14.

other human being is the enemy. He is not able to simply go on living as if nothing had happened, and indeed he does not, for even after the war, he is haunted by his crimes. He is not one of those Japanese who are able to "swing from one behavior to another without psychic cost" as described by Ruth Benedict.[82]

Perhaps this is a cheap defense of the Japanese, tantamount to saying, "Sure, most of us are completely amoral, but there are a few of us who aren't so bad!" but such a reading of *Yellow Man* and *The Sea and Poison* would be too simplistic. It would appear that Endō is indeed protesting against Ruth Benedict's descriptions of the Japanese people. He uses her characterizations of the Japanese and points out that, while they may apply generally as overall tendencies, it would be false to say that all Japanese have no concept of sin, that all Japanese have no conscience, and that the only thing guiding their moral choices is the fear of external sanction.[83]

§ 6. A MORE NUANCED VIEW OF THE WESTERNER

So what about the other side? What about the white people, who, according to Durand in *Yellow Man*, are essentially different from the Japanese? Are they really so different? Durand would seem to say so, for he fails in his attempt to become like the Japanese in being indifferent to

---

[82] Benedict, 138.

[83] Whether Ruth Benedict really meant to judge Japanese people in this way is debatable, and I would side with those who say that she did not. After all, she did not write that Japanese morality is completely based on shame and that Japanese have no such thing as guilt, but that, in Japan, the *emphasis* falls on shame rather than guilt. Nevertheless, her work is often oversimplified and interpreted as saying that Japanese have no guilt and no conscience, and it is the reception of her work to which Endō appears to be reacting.

God. With other characters, however, the differences become a bit more ambiguous.

Besides the murdered American prisoners, who don't have much of a chance to act or voice their opinions on anything, there is only one white character in *The Sea and Poison*, namely Dr. Hashimoto's German wife Hilda. Within the story itself, she comes across very strongly as being "the other." She is tall, has fair skin and walks around with long, masculine strides. Having worked as a nurse in Germany before coming to Japan, she helps out when she can, but does so in such a culturally insensitive manner that she invites more disdain than appreciation. The differences between her and the Japanese characters even spill over into the economic realm. She still has access to rare goods like soap and sugar while the Japanese characters must do without. Endō sets her up as being completely different from those around her, and the difference in the realm of morality comes to the fore in a scene with the Japanese Nurse Ueda.

All the doctors, interns and other nurses are busy with an operation, and Nurse Ueda is left to watch over the other patients. One of them has a spontaneous pneumothorax. He needs immediate medical attention, so she telephones Dr. Asai, who is preoccupied with the surgery. Irritated, he tells her to just give the patient some anesthetic and let him die since he isn't going to make it anyway. She rushes to the patient with a needle of anesthetic in her hand, and finds Hilda there with the patient. Hilda sees the needle, realizes what Nurse Ueda is about to do, and violently shoves her away. After Hilda administers emergency aid to the patient, she and Ueda have the following exchange of words:

"Why did you try to give him an injection?" asked Hilda, reprimanding me [Nurse Ueda] as she stood in the doorway with her arms crossed like a man. "You were trying to kill him, weren't you? I know that's what you were trying to do."

"But..." I answered in an exhausted voice, with my eyes cast down on the floor, "This patient was going to die soon anyway. Isn't it more merciful to give him a painless death?"

"Even if he was going to die, nobody has the right to kill!" said Hilda, slamming her hand down on the desk. "Don't you fear God!? Don't you believe in the wrath of God!?"[84]

All ethical questions about euthanasia aside, there are two interesting points here. First, that Hilda refers to the fear of God in her scolding of Nurse Ueda, and second, that Hilda is German.

For Hilda, euthanasia is unquestionably wrong. She operates in a system of absolute morality – one of Ruth Benedict's "guilt cultures" – and it is based on her belief in God. When Hilda yells at Nurse Ueda, asking whether she fears God or not, the implication is of course that Nurse Ueda does not, and it is because she does not fear God that she can even contemplate committing this awful crime. Once again, there is the image of the godless Japanese, who by virtue of being godless, is also amoral and has no conscience.

But why did Endō choose to give Hilda a German identity? Hilda could just as easily have been a Japanese woman, but Endō seems to want to make a point of juxtaposing the Japanese Nurse Ueda with a Westerner. If he had wanted to simply use any white character, he could have chosen someone from any number of other countries. In almost all his other works set in the 20th century, Endō uses

---

[84] Endō, *The Sea and Poison*, 113.

French people as the white characters. He does so in *White Man, Yellow Man, Wonderful Fool*, and *Deep River*. This makes sense, as Endō's original field of study was French literature, and he knew about France and the French people after studying at the University of Lyon from 1950 to 1953. Choosing to make Hilda a German woman seems to be an intentional choice, especially considering the time frame in which the novel takes place (World War II), the subject of Hilda's argument with Nurse Ueda (euthanasia), and the general theme of the book (human experimentation).

At exactly the same time that Hilda is berating Nurse Ueda for her attempted euthanasia of her patient, her fellow Germans on the other side of the world were doing the same thing to thousands of disabled people. Germany was, of course, a white nation with a Western "guilt culture." Though Nazi ideology was atheistic, German culture had a long tradition of belief in a monotheistic God – the same God Hilda evokes. In addition to euthanasia, German doctors like Dr. Josef Mengele experimented on thousands of people in the concentration camps, just as Hilda's husband Dr. Hashimoto is about to do to the American prisoner. For Hilda to talk about nobody having a right to kill and evoking belief in God's wrath as if that would stop people from committing such heinous acts therefore begins to ring hollow.

This is of course not a simple, childish, "You did it too" defense of Japanese atrocities in the war. Endō is clearly very disturbed by the evil his compatriots committed and does not seek to excuse any of it. What he does seem to object to is the idea that Japanese are in some way different, or more prone to acts of evil than Westerners. Japanese and Westerners are, in fact, not so different. This idea comes across even stronger if one compares *The Sea and Poison* and *Yellow Man* with the latter's companion novella *White Man*.

At first glance, *White Man* seems to further illustrate the extent of the difference between white and yellow people. Taking place in Lyon, France during the Second World War, all of its characters are white Europeans. As one would expect, they inhabit a world of sharply distinguished dualisms, not the ambiguities of the Japanese world. The story itself is a classic tale of Good versus Evil, pitting the evil and nameless protagonist against the good characters of Jacques and Marie-Thérèse. The almost revoltingly evil protagonist is a sadist and Nazi collaborator working in a Gestapo interrogation center. Jacques is a priest and a member of the French Resistance. He is very close to the young nun, Marie-Thérèse. Indeed, he is almost like an older brother to her. The three knew each other before the war when they were students in university.

The story ends in a climactic clash between good and evil, with astonishing acts of heroic self-sacrifice on the parts of the good characters. The Gestapo capture Jacques, and the protagonist helps to torture him for information on the Resistance. The protagonist decides to use Marie-Thérèse against Jacques by having her brought to the interrogation center and threatening to have her raped, and thus destroyed as a social person, if Jacques doesn't give up his Resistance comrades. Just when it looks like evil is about to triumph, Marie-Thérèse willingly gives herself over to the protagonist and allows him to rape her so that Jacques is no longer in the position of holding her fate in his hands. At the same time, Jacques commits suicide by biting off and swallowing his own tongue so that he cannot betray the Resistance. Marie-Thérèse has sacrificed her virginity for Jacques, and Jacques, having committed the unforgivable sin of suicide, has sacrificed both his life and his soul for the Resistance.

This is truly a story of a dramatic, dualistic battle between good and evil, seemingly impossible for the Japanese who, according to Chiba, have no drama within themselves[85] and cannot distinguish between extremes like light and darkness.[86] Nevertheless, when it comes to lived experience, there are significant points of contact and similarity between the white characters in *White Man* and the yellow characters in *Yellow Man* and *The Sea and Poison*.

The first is fatigue. Although Chiba in *Yellow Man* describes his fatigue as a particularly "yellow" characteristic,[87] white characters in *White Man* suffer from it as well. The protagonist expresses this "deep fatigue" in two instances. The first time is after he tries to take advantage of Marie-Thérèse at their university ball. As he looks at her crumpled body, he describes how, "Something desolate tightened around my chest. I don't know why. It wouldn't call it sadness, but fatigue. A terribly deep fatigue."[88] He experiences this fatigue again after raping Marie-Thérèse in the Gestapo interrogation center and hearing that Jacques has committed suicide. "Something began to tighten around my chest," he says. "I tasted this same sadness at Hotel Le Hameau in that instant after I subdued Marie-Thérèse. I wouldn't call it sorrow or desolation. Perhaps sadness isn't the right word either. It's closer to a deep fatigue."[89]

---

[85] Endō, *White Man, Yellow Man*, 90.

[86] Endō, *White Man, Yellow Man*, 161.

[87] Endō, *White Man, Yellow Man*, 91. "A yellow person like me doesn't have these serious, exaggerated things like consciousness of sin and nihilism. Not like you [white people]. I don't have any of that in me at all. All I have is fatigue. This deep fatigue."

[88] Endō, *White Man, Yellow Man*, 45.

The protagonist is not the only white person to suffer from Chiba's "yellow" fatigue. The protagonist's Gestapo boss, a German lieutenant, is perpetually drowsy. Quite significantly, the protagonist draws a connection between the lieutenant's fatigue and the horrible abuse they carry out when they torture people. One day, the lieutenant walks into the office looking as exhausted as usual. The protagonist remarks, "I could tell by looking at his disposition that there would be an interrogation session today. The lieutenant always had this listless expression on his face before beginning torture."[90]

The German lieutenant also exhibits another characteristic seen in two minor characters in *The Sea and Poison*, namely, the ability to swing from committing extreme acts of evil to doing completely normal, peaceful things without "psychic cost." One evening, the protagonist finds the lieutenant playing a piano in an abandoned mansion. The usually languid lieutenant suddenly looks alive, and cheerfully tells the protagonist about his love for Mozart and how he plays music with his wife and children when he's not being called up for duties.[91] This lieutenant swings back and forth between being a Gestapo torturer and a normal, music-loving family man. In this regard, he is much like the petrol station owner and clothing boutique owner in the opening of *The Sea and Poison* who are both war criminals and normal, cheerful, small-business owners. If the Japanese characters in *The Sea and Poison* are *bukimi*, so is this German lieutenant.

---

[89] Endō, *White Man, Yellow Man*, 83.

[90] Endō, *White Man, Yellow Man*, 65.

[91] Endō, *White Man, Yellow Man*, 64.

Finally, there is Endō's much-discussed image of the "mud swamp." In his historical novels, *Silence* and *The Samurai*, Endō describes Japan as a "mud swamp" in which it is impossible for Christianity to take root and grow. Interestingly, Endō uses the image of the mud swamp in both *White Man* and *Yellow Man*, eleven years before publishing *Silence* and, in both cases, he uses it to describe non-Japanese French characters as they sink into sin. When the protagonist of *White Man* rapes Marie-Thérèse, he describes how "Hot steam rose up from the bottom of the mud swamp."[92] When Durand describes his first sexual act with Kimiko in *Yellow Man*, he likewise uses the image of the mud swamp, saying "I let my legs slide into the bottomless mud swamp of lust."[93] It seems like the swamp, which European characters in Endō's later works use to describe the entire nation of Japan, is also present within white people.

§ 7. CONCLUSION

In the first period of his literary career, Endō constructs his anthropological model of the Japanese person. Looking at this model, it can be difficult to see how theological dialogue between East and West could possibly begin. How can one speak of sin to someone who has absolutely no concept of the matter? How can one speak about light and darkness to someone who sees everything in a haze of gray? How can one talk about guilt to someone who understands only shame? It could seem like the gulf is unbridgeable.

Endō's characters, however, are not limited to thought and speech. They also feel and do, and it is at this level of

---

[92] Endō, *White Man, Yellow Man*, 81.

[93] Endō, *White Man, Yellow Man*, 149.

emotion and real action that the differences between white and yellow begin to appear less clear. Despite everything they say about themselves and each other, their actions and raw intuitions are often quite similar, suggesting, perhaps, that white and yellow aren't quite so radically different after all. Perhaps dialogue is possible.

CHAPTER II: JAPANESE RESPONSES TO CHRISTIANITY

The second period of Endō's career is bookended by two monumental works of historical fiction: *Silence*, published in 1966, and *The Samurai*, published in 1980. The two works share many similarities in setting, plot and theme. Both are based on real events, set in the 17th century, feature Christian missionaries as main characters, and deal with the problem of spreading the Christian message in Japan. Though the events in the novels take place over 250 years ago, many of their themes are still relevant today.

Whereas in discussing the first period in Endō's literary career we looked primarily at some of his questions on who the Japanese person is, we will focus in this section on the religious response of Japanese characters to the Christian message. As in the last section, we will look first at what characters say about the deficient religiosity of Japanese people, and then demonstrate how their actual lived experiences, their feelings and their actions run contrary to what people, especially Western characters, say about them.

§1. SILENCE

Published in 1966, *Silence* is the most famous and widely-read of Endō's novels, not only in Japan, but especially overseas. It has generated much controversy over its portrayal of apostate priests and a Christ who seems to encourage apostasy. It also seems to argue that Christianity will never succeed in taking root in Japan. This is the issue we would like to discuss in this section of our paper.

A. Historical Background

As it is a historical novel, a brief sketch of the circumstances surrounding the plot would be in order. The so-called "Christian Century" in Japan began in 1549 when St. Francis Xavier and a group of Jesuit missionaries first landed on the Japanese archipelago. Missionizing efforts were initially quite successful, with a number of Japanese feudal lords (*daimyo*) converting along with all the people in their territories. The missionaries began setting up seminaries to train native Japanese priests, and they even received their own pieces of land. The Christian population of Japan grew steadily, reaching 300,000 by the beginning of the 16th century, and possibly even 760,000 by the 1630s, at a time when Japan's total population is estimated at approximately 12 million.[94] It is therefore possible that Japan's Christian population could one day have amounted to over 6% of the total population. By comparison, Japan's Christian population today amounts to under 1% (one million out of 127 million).

The initial success of the mission in Japan would soon be reversed, however, as the leaders of Japan became increasingly suspicious of the missionaries. Hideyoshi Toyotomi, the most powerful ruler in Japan at the end of the 16th century, began to suspect that the missionaries were the vanguard of an incoming Iberian invasion. Persecution began in 1587 when Hideyoshi ordered Christian missionaries to leave the country, and flared up in 1597 with the crucifixions of the now canonized Twenty-Six Martyrs. A power-grab

---

[94] Kentarō Miyazaki, "Roman Catholic Mission in Pre-Modern Japan," in *Handbook of Christianity in Japan (Handbook of Oriental Studies Section 5: Japan)*, vol. 10, ed. Mark R. Mullins (Leiden: Brill Academic Publishing, 2003), 6.

followed Hideyoshi's death in 1598, resulting in the establishment of the Tokugawa dynasty that would rule Japan from 1603 to 1868. The Tokugawa government pronounced an edict banning Christianity in 1614, initiating a brutal period of persecution that would not end until the second half of the 19th century. Under the threat of torture or death, Christians were forced to apostasize, often by stepping on images of Jesus Christ or Mary called *fumie* (literally meaning "step-on picture"). Starting in 1633, the Tokugawa government closed Japan off from all external contact under the *sakoku* (literally "locked country") policy of national isolation. No foreigners were allowed to enter Japanese ports, with the exception of a few Dutch and Chinese traders who were allowed to enter Nagasaki.[95] The Christians who had not abandoned their faith were cut off from all contact with the wider church and had no priests to administer the Sacraments. They would remain isolated until 1853, when the "Black Ships" of the United States Navy forced the government to open its ports.

B. THE CHARGES AGAINST JAPANESE CHRISTIANS IN *SILENCE*

It is against this backdrop that the story of *Silence* takes place. The novel begins in 1632. News reaches Rome that Cristovao Ferreira, a Portuguese Jesuit who has worked as a missionary in Japan for over twenty years, has committed apostasy. His former students Francis Garrpe and Sebastian Rodrigo cannot believe that their teacher would abandon the faith even under the most terrible torture, so they head to Japan to find out what happened. The novel largely takes the

---

[95] Even the Dutch and Chinese were, however, not actually allowed on Japanese soil. The government constructed a small man-made island called Dejima just off the shore, and foreign traders were only allowed there.

form of letters written by Rodrigo to his congregation in Portugal, describing his experiences.

After a long and arduous journey, the two priests eventually make it to Japan and find some small communities of believers. They begin their pastoral work and, initially, things go quite well, so much so that Rodrigo even begins to wonder whether the reports of the severity of the persecution in Japan were not exaggerated. Such illusions are quickly shattered, however, as officials get wind of their presence in the area and begin a manhunt. Though they separate to avoid having both of them get caught at the same time, both Rodrigo and Garrpe are soon captured. Garrpe and several Japanese Christians are martyred, but Rodrigo is kept alive. He meets his former mentor Ferreira who tells him that it is impossible to plant Christianity in the "mud swamp" of Japan, not due to the vicious and effective persecution, but because of certain deficiencies in the Japanese people. The climax of the novel comes when Rodrigo is presented with an unimaginably awful choice. A number of Japanese Christians are subjected to the agonizing torture of *anadzuri* (being suspended upside down in a pit), and will not be released unless Rodrigo steps on a *fumie* and apostatizes. Ferreira convinces him that the greatest act of love in this situation – the choice that Christ himself would have taken – is to apostatize. Rodrigo hears Christ speaking to him from the *fumie*, giving him permission to apostatize for the sake of the tortured peasants. Rodrigo complies, feeling a dull pain reverberate through his leg as he tramples the most beautiful and holy face he's ever known – the image of Jesus.

In addition to a dramatic storyline with gripping scenes of martyrdom and torturous descriptions of human suffering, much of the novel consists of a series of dialogues between

Sebastian Rodrigo and his adversaries. The majority of the text is written in the first person from Rodrigo's perspective, so the reader gets intimate insights into his thoughts and feelings. Through these dialogues and glimpses into Rodrigo's thoughts, Endō describes the Japanese person and even the entire country of Japan as fundamentally incompatible with the Christian faith.

Rodrigo encounters Japanese Christians first-hand, and though he's glad to serve them, he can't help but feel troubled by certain aspects of their spirituality. Before being captured, he goes to a small fishing village on Gotō Island to teach, baptize, hear confessions and so on. As he's about to leave, the villagers ask him for crucifixes, icons and other tangible objects. Having nothing else to give them, he takes apart his rosary and gives them the beads. As he does so, he thinks to himself, "It isn't necessarily bad that the Japanese believers revere these things, but I still get this strange sense of unease. It feels like they're getting something wrong."[96] He appears to be concerned that the Japanese Christians misunderstand the use of icons and other religious objects, perhaps even engaging in idol worship.

He has a similar experience after his capture as well. A small group of Japanese Christians is held captive together with him. He speaks to one of them, a woman who introduces herself by her baptismal name of Monica. He mentions that they might be killed, and she responds by describing her understanding of Paradise. She has been taught that Heaven is a place of eternal comfort where she will be free of brutal tax collections, hunger, disease and toil. Rodrigo's immediate reaction is to want to tell her that, "Paradise doesn't exist in the way that you think it does," but he manages to hold his

[96] Endō, *Silence*, 67.

tongue. He thinks to himself that, "These peasants think of Heaven in the same way as children undergoing catechesis. They're dreaming, seeing Heaven as a separate world with no toil and heavy taxes."[97] The Japanese believers, though sincere, have incorrect understandings of Catholic doctrine. They believe they are adhering properly to the Christian faith, but they are actually not.

Ferreira confirms this idea in his first dialogue with Rodrigo. Ferreira describes Japan as a mud swamp in which it is impossible for Christianity to take root. Rodrigo protests, saying, "But churches were erected all over this country when you first came here. The faith at this time had the fresh fragrance of morning flowers, and large numbers of Japanese received baptism like the Jews who gathered at the River Jordan." Ferreira responds that,

> The one to whom the Japanese were praying in the churches we built was not the Christian God. They had distorted it into a god that we cannot understand. If you call that thing "God," then... No. That is not God. It's like a butterfly caught in a spider web. At first, the butterfly is unmistakably still a butterfly. The next day, it still looks like a butterfly, at least from the outside. It still has the wings and thorax, but it has lost its true essence and is now an empty shell. In Japan, our God was just like a butterfly caught in a spider web. It still looked like our God from the outside, but had lost its true essence, and was nothing but an empty shell.[98]

---

[97] Endō, *Silence*, 129.

[98] Endō, *Silence*, 235.

Rodrigo counters that he has personally witnessed the martyrdoms of Japanese Christians aflame with faith, to which Ferreira reiterates his point, saying,

> The god they believed in was not the Christian God. To this day, the Japanese have never had the concept of God, and they will never have it. [...] The Japanese do not have the ability to conceive of a god completely separate from human beings. The Japanese are incapable of imagining anything beyond the human being.[99]

Ferreira makes very clear that not only do Japanese Christians have a deficient faith, they are also incapable of developing a more "correct" understanding of God. It is not a question of pedagogy or catechesis, but a question of an inherent incapacity of the Japanese to understand the Christian concept of God.

These are, of course, the views of outsiders – foreigners such as Ferreira and Rodrigo – but Japanese characters also express pessimistic attitudes regarding both the receptivity of Japanese to Christianity and the prospects for its growth. Rodrigo's interpreter, a Japanese man and former seminarian, describes Christianity as an *arigata meiwaku* – an unwanted, unneeded gift that is in fact an annoying inconvenience made doubly annoying because one is supposed to be thankful for it.[100] To the Japanese, Christianity is what one might call a "white elephant" in English. The magistrate Lord Inoue, also a former Christian, expresses similar sentiments when he compares the priests' missionary efforts to the unwelcome affections of an ugly woman. Alternatively, he says that Christianity could be

---

[99] Endō, *Silence*, 236.

[100] Endō, *Silence*, 138.

compared to a barren woman who, by virtue of being unable to bear children, has no right to become anybody's wife.[101] Christianity is, in other words, unsuitable to Japan. Like Ferreira, these two Japanese characters say that the problem does not lie with how Christianity was brought to Japan, but that it was brought at all. They seem to argue for an inherent incompatibility between their homeland and this foreign religion.

After Rodrigo commits apostasy, Lord Inoue comes to visit him. "You didn't lose to me, padre," he says, "You were defeated by this mud swamp called Japan."[102] Lord Inoue reveals that he is aware of peasants on Gotō Island and Ikitsuki who still call themselves Christians, but he sees no need to apprehend them. Echoing Ferreira, he explains that there's no need to do so, as they will inevitably warp Christianity into something completely unrecognizable. He lets out a deep sigh and says, "That's just how Japan is. There's nothing to be done about it."[103]

According to the characters in Silence, then, Japanese soil is almost toxic to Christianity. Japanese people are simply unable to accept the faith, and those that do accept it will inadvertently distort or misunderstand it. The Roman Catholic Church wasted its time missionizing in the 16th and 17th centuries, and as these deficiencies of the Japanese are an inherent part of the national character, all Christian denominations today are wasting their time when they missionize.

---

[101] Endō, Silence, 192.

[102] Endō, Silence, 288.

[103] Endō, Silence, 290.

It is important, however, to note that the pessimistic statements were all given either by Western characters or Japanese apostates. The lived experience of the Japanese faithful paints a remarkably different picture.

C. IN DEFENSE OF JAPANESE CHRISTIANS IN *SILENCE*

First, there is the issue of martyrdom. Going through the novel, one counts at least twelve Christians who are killed for their faith.[104] Of these twelve martyrs, only Garrpe is a Westerner, and the rest are Japanese. Other Westerners withstand torture for the sake of the faith,[105] but none bear the ultimate witness of martyrdom. How can Rodrigo, Ferreira, Inoue and others still make the case that the Japanese Christians' faith was deficient? They claim that, even if Japanese Christians died for their faith, they actually had an incorrect understanding of faith. This accusation, however, brings up other questions.

As mentioned above, Rodrigo senses unease with the way the Japanese Christians live out their faith and (mis)understand Christian doctrine. It appears that they do indeed harbor rather simplistic views of salvation and perhaps do not quite understand the difference between an icon and an idol. The question at this point is, however, whether one *needs* to have a completely "correct" understanding of orthodox doctrine in order to be a Christian.

---

[104] There are thirteen if one also counts a prisoner who dies of heat stroke while in captivity. The others are Mokichi and Ichizō (killed by water cruficixion), the "one-eyed man" (beheaded), Garrpe (drowned), Monica (drowned), two other Japanese peasants (drowned), a family of four as recounted in a Dutch merchant's log, and the priest Thomas Araki whose fate is also recorded in the Dutch merchant's log.

[105] The six Westerners (and one Japanese) tortured with hot water at Unzen in the beginning of the novel.

If the Japanese Christians placed too much value on tangible objects of worship such as icons and crosses, couldn't one also say the same thing about many contemporaneous 17th century European Christians? Even if Japanese Christians like Monica understand Paradise solely in temporal terms, couldn't one say the same thing about many Western Christians even today? And as much as Rodrigo sees problems with the Japanese Christians' faith, are there not deficiencies in his own faith?

Endō gives his readers a clue that Rodrigo's understanding of Christ is in fact very much culturally bound. Whenever he prays, Rodrigo tries to visualize Christ's face. At one such moment, he describes Christ's face in the following way: "Those clear, blue eyes gazed at me as if to console me. The face was calm, but overflowing with confidence."[106] The description of Christ's eyes as "blue" is clearly intentional. With this clue, Endō demonstrates how Rodrigo has a completely Eurocentric understanding of Christ, which, historically speaking, is simply wrong – a fact of which Endō was undoubtedly fully aware.[107] How can Rodrigo speak of a universal gospel when he himself has limited Christ to a European identity?[108] And how can Rodrigo criticize Japanese

---

[106] Endō, *Silence*, 166.

[107] The amount of research Endō has done for this and other novels indicates a strong knowledge of history, art history, philosophy and theology. It would be highly unlikely for him to be completely unaware of research into the Historical Jesus and historical-critical biblical scholarship of his time. He even wrote his own historically researched *A Life of Jesus* in 1973, which draws heavily on the latest scholarly research into the historical Jesus available at the time..

[108] Endō makes similar criticisms of European Christians in his earlier work *Yellow Man*, in which Chiba describes how, as a child, he learned from his French priest that "God is a white man with blond hair," and a "foreigner"

Christians for incorrect understandings of Christ when his own understanding of Christ is so limited to his European perspective?

Perhaps the greatest example of faith in the entire novel lies not with the trained priest Rodrigo, but with the faint-hearted Japanese peasant Kichijirō. Kichijirō is a coward, apostatizing several times while others, including his siblings, are martyred. He plays the role of Judas to Rodrigo, betraying the latter to the government authorities. Nevertheless, despite his crimes and his incurable cowardice, he repents, confesses his sins, and follows Rodrigo to the end of the priest's life. While Rodrigo continuously looks down on Kichijirō and other Japanese Christians, and somewhat self-righteously thanks God for allowing him to share in the suffering of Christ, Kichijirō honestly confesses his own cowardice and weakness to God, asking why he must suffer. It almost seems as if the entire relationship between Rodrigo and Kichijirō is less that of Christ and Judas (as Rodrigo seems to assume), but more like that of the righteous Pharisee and the sinful tax collector from Luke 18.

Throughout *Silence*, there seems to be a sharp distinction between what is said and what is done, or alternatively, how people are described and how they actually are. Both the Europeans and the Japanese have almost no confidence in the faith of the Japanese peasants, and yet, these are the ones who die and suffer for the faith. Unlike the missionaries and their captors, the peasants are largely silent. They do not have much of a voice, but through their living witness, they contradict much of what is said about them, challenging the

(p. 92). The theme of Europeans appropriating Christ for themselves comes up again in *Deep River* when French seminarians tell the Japanese seminarian Ōtsu that "God grew up in our world – the European world you dislike so much" (p. 310).

idea that Japanese are inherently unable to become proper Christians.

§ 2. *THE SAMURAI*

Similar issues come up in *The Samurai*. Roughly contemporaneous with the events that take place in *Silence*, the novel chronicles the first Japanese mission to the West, and features two main protagonists – the arrogant and ambitious Franciscan missionary Velasco and the stoic and loyal samurai Rokuemon Hasekura.

Seeking to establish trade and diplomatic ties with Nueva España, the Tokugawa government sends a diplomatic mission of four low-ranking samurai across the Pacific Ocean, together with their retainers and a group of Japanese merchants. Velasco joins them as their interpreter. Velasco has two goals: to get himself appointed as bishop of Japan and to win exclusive missionizing rights for the Franciscan order. He continuously manipulates both the Japanese and European sides in order to accomplish these goals. The journey takes Hasekura, Velasco and the rest of the mission to the Spanish colonies of Nueva España, Spain itself, and ultimately to Rome where the envoys meet Pope Paul V. Along the way, the merchants, three of the four envoys and Hasekura's retainer, Yozō, convert to Christianity, though purely for reasons of expedience and not out of any genuine faith. Just as it looks as though both Velasco and the envoys are going to succeed in their respective missions, they receive word that the Tokugawa government has abandoned its plans of trading with Nueva España and has intensified its persecution of Christians. Unable to fulfill their missions, the men must return to a closed Japan that has become dangerously hostile to their new Christian religion.

Roughly half of the story is told from the perspective of the missionary Velasco, with the other half showing the perspective of the samurai Hasekura. Endō thus gives the reader both a Western and a Japanese perspective. Like *Silence*, much of the novel also consists of dialogues and debates in which characters debate the question of whether or not it is possible to bring Christianity into Japan. Endō restates some of the ideas earlier expressed in *Silence*, such as the inability of Japanese to conceive of anything transcendent and the incompleteness of the faith of those who do convert.

A. THE CHARGES AGAINST JAPANESE CHRISTIANS IN *THE SAMURAI*

After working as a missionary in Japan for ten years, Velasco appears to be somewhat baffled by the Japanese who, despite possessing "a degree of intelligence and curiosity as developed as any European nation, close their eyes and stick their fingers in their ears in all matters concerning our [Christian] God."[109] Sometimes he gets the feeling that for the Japanese, "the only definition of happiness is to gain profit in the temporal world. The Japanese will pounce on any religion that has worldly benefits as its goal, such as acquiring riches, winning wars and curing disease. When it comes to the supernatural or the infinite, however, they are completely indifferent."[110] Christianity, with its transcendent God and tendency to focus on a reality beyond the temporal, is of no interest to them. There is, in fact, "a vast gulf separating their

---

[109] Endō, *The Samurai*, 78.

[110] Endō, *The Samurai*, 84.

[Japanese] faith from what we Christians call 'faith.'"[111] Velasco repeats this observation several times throughout the novel, and has it confirmed by other experienced missionaries and even the Japanese themselves. For example, Velasco asks one of the merchants if he would like to learn the deeper significance of the Mass. The merchant replies directly and completely unashamedly that "Japanese merchants will adopt anything they find useful. If it should be beneficial to learn Christian doctrine on this voyage, then why not?"[112] There is no question of faith here, just pragmatism and profit.

Velasco decides to take advantage of the merchants' willingness to adopt anything that will profit them, and tells them that the Spanish will only trade with fellow Christians. Eager to do business, the merchants convert. One of the Japanese envoys, a samurai called Matsuki, criticizes Velasco for his unethical proselytization. He warns Velasco that the Japanese merchants and politicians will only make themselves open to the Christian faith as long as it profits them to do so, and they will abandon it as soon as it ceases to be beneficial.[113] Velasco responds that his methods are justified because God will work within the merchants no matter what their original motivations for conversion were. "Once the seeds have been sown, they have been sown," he says.[114] In some mysterious way, God will manifest Godself in their lives and demonstrate God's existence. Matsuki disagrees and rejects Velasco's optimism, saying that, "Deus cannot demonstrate his [*sic*]

---

[111] Endō, *The Samurai*, 96.

[112] Endō, *The Samurai*, 95.

[113] Endō, *The Samurai*, 102.

[114] Endō, *The Samurai*, 103.

existence in the lives of those merchants [...] because they do not care whether Deus exists or not. And it's not just them. Japanese people in general are like that."[115]

These ideas – that the Japanese are incapable of conceiving anything beyond the temporal, seek only worldly profit and will abandon Christianity as soon as it ceases to be beneficial – are further emphasized by the Jesuit missionary Valente, who, after thirty years of mission work in Japan, has concluded that, "of all the people in the world, none are as unsuited to [the Christian] faith as the Japanese."[116] Like Velasco, he has learned that the Japanese have a fundamental insensibility to all absolutes that transcend humankind and nature. They understand that the world is fleeting, much like Christians do, but rather than seeing this as a cause for despair, they revel in the transience and do not seek salvation in anything absolute. Japanese never move beyond the temporal realm, and are thus incapable of understanding the Christian God. A bishop asks Valente how this could be if the Church at one time counted 400,000 believers in Japan. What did these converts believe? Valente responds, "I don't know. As soon as the emperor banned Christianity, half of them evaporated like the mist." He explains that even those who appeared to have strong faith left the Church, seemingly without any qualms or misgivings.[117] As Matsuki warned, the Japanese abandoned Christianity as soon as it ceased to be an asset and became instead a liability.

These characterizations of the Japanese attitude towards the transcendent in general and Christianity in particular fit

---

[115] Endō, *The Samurai*, 104.

[116] Endō, *The Samurai*, 246.

[117] Endō, *The Samurai*, 247, 248.

some of the Japanese characters perfectly. Once it becomes evident that the mission has failed, the envoys completely cease participating in Christian rituals. They had converted to Christianity solely for the sake of their mission, and once the mission is over, they seemingly shed their Christian robes with ease. Likewise, the merchants also quickly and painlessly recant their Christian faith. Of all those who converted, only Yozō, Hasekura's loyal servant, continues attending Mass. It seems that Velasco was wrong, and God does not work mysteriously within the hearts of all those who have come into contact with God.

As is the case with *Silence*, however, a look into the lived experiences of the Japanese characters shows a different story. Endō does not dispute the difficulty that Japanese have in trying to conceptualize a radically transcendent being like the Christian God, but he does take issue with the charge that Japanese are incapable of developing any sort of Christian faith. Most of the Japanese converts do indeed seem to shed their Christian faith as painlessly as taking off one's coat, but at least three characters develop a deep bond with Christ.

B. In Defense of Japanese Christians in *The Samurai*

The first is Hasekura's servant, Yozō. Whether he is able to accept the idea of a radically transcendent God or not is never made clear and is in fact irrelevant to his journey of faith. Yozō's conversion has nothing to do with either intellectual assent or any desire for worldly benefit. Yozō is touched first and foremost by a simple act of personal kindness. As the envoys' ship sails towards Nueva España, it runs into a storm. Yozō's clothes and bedding end up completely soaked, and he is completely at a loss. Velasco sees how distressed Yozō is and kindly shares his own clothes and bedding with him.[118] This simple gesture has a profound effect on Yozō, and from then on, he begins moving slowly towards the Christian faith. He asks Velasco to pray for a dead comrade, and then asks him to teach him about the Christian faith. When Hasekura decides to convert, Yozō expresses his desire to also receive baptism. Once it is clear that the mission has failed and the other converts stop attending Mass, Yozō still goes faithfully. When the envoys return to Japan, it becomes clear to them how dangerous it is for them to be Christian. Nevertheless, Yozō makes an explicit confession of faith to his master Hasekura.[119] He later professes his conviction that this Christ he believes in will always remain with him. His faith is not in any transcendent being existing beyond the natural world, but in the figure of Christ as the ever-present companion. It is an intimate, personal faith of relationship initially awakened by intimate, personal acts of kindness.

The second person is the Japanese monk living with a Tecali tribe in Nueva España. He explains to Hasekura that he was born in Japan, but lost both of his parents to war. Some Christian missionaries took him in as a servant. When persecutions became severe, they sent him to a seminary in the Philippines. He became a monk, but was never able to get along with any of the priests in any of the monasteries or seminaries, whether in the Philippines or in Nueva España. He eventually left the monasteries to go and live with the indigenous Tecali *indios*. He is disillusioned with the priests who preach a God of love and compassion while allowing the Spanish army to rob the *indios* of their land and lives. Despite

[118] Endō, *The Samurai*, 100.

[119] Endō, *The Samurai*, 378.

his disillusionment with the clergy, he remains a Christian. His faith is in the Jesus who lives among the poor *indios*, not the Jesus of the palatial cathedrals.[120] The Jesus he believes in is the wretched, weak and ugly Christ who understands the suffering of the weak.[121] Like Yozō, this monk's faith is not motivated by personal gain. When it comes to the question of transcendence, whether or not this monk has the ability to conceptualize the transcendent is not addressed, but he would have difficulty believing in a strong, beautiful and distant Jesus. "If that person were so high up that we couldn't reach him," he says, "and if he lived a life of strength and nobility, I don't think I would have been able to feel this way about him."[122]

Unlike Yozō and the monk, Hasekura does convert for more worldly reasons. Velasco tells him that converting will make the mission run smoother, and though Hasekura vehemently opposes conversion at first, he eventually complies. Once the mission has failed, however, he stops attending Mass. On the surface, he appears to be just like all the Japanese described by Velasco, Valente and Matsuki, but, in reality, his relationship to Christ goes far deeper. Throughout the story, both before and after his baptism, Hasekura encounters several crucifixes bearing the image of Christ. He cannot understand how the Westerners could possibly worship this weak, emaciated and powerless figure and, at first, is convinced that Christianity is a dangerous and heretical sect. This man they call "Lord" is nothing like his own lord who wields power and lives in a castle.[123]

[120] Endō, *The Samurai*, 175-177.

[121] Endō, *The Samurai*, 338, 339.

[122] Endō, *The Samurai*, 338.

Hasekura's bewilderment never seems to subside, but rather than simply ignore the Cross, he continues asking what the meaning of Christianity is. He seems in fact to be struggling with St. Paul's characterization of the crucified Christ as "a stumbling block to Jews and foolishness to Gentiles."[124] He is engaged in a genuine struggle with the shockingly radical statement of the Cross. Far from being incapable of receiving the gospel message, the mere fact that he continues to struggle throughout the novel, even entering into conversation with the Crucified,[125] indicates some sort of real relationship with Christ.

Hasekura's questioning and his own views on the Crucified begin to change towards the end of the novel. On the way back to Japan, he meets the monk in Nueva España again, and asks him how he can worship "this ugly, emaciated man." The narrator writes that, "For the first time, the Samurai asked this question in earnest."[126] The question is no longer a rhetorical one of ridicule, but a genuine one of inquiry. When he returns to Japan only to be treated with contempt by his superiors, he even begins to identify with the suffering and powerless Christ.[127] The greatest indication of his move towards faith comes at his execution. As he walks towards his fate, Yozō says to him, "From this point... he will be with you. From this point on... he will attend to you." Hasekura says nothing, but "nods firmly."[128] "He" is a clear

---

[123] Endō, *The Samurai*, 118.

[124] 1 Cor 1:23.

[125] Endō, *The Samurai*, 262.

[126] Endō, *The Samurai*, 338.

[127] Endō, *The Samurai*, 373.

reference to Christ.[129] Endō doesn't clarify whether Hasekura has come to full belief in Christ at this point, but the trajectory of his relationship with Christ up to this point seems to indicate that his nod was one of affirmation and faith.

§ 3. CONCLUSION

In *The Samurai*, as in *Silence* European missionaries have little faith in the ability of Japanese people to develop any genuine Christian faith. Just as in *Yellow Man* and *The Sea and Poison*, there are certain concepts crucial to developing a Christian sensitivity that Japanese people are completely incapable of learning. Nevertheless, Japanese characters in both novels do come to believe. Their faith may be immature, but what Christian can rightly say that his or her faith is not incomplete? Furthermore, the characters of Yozō, the monk, and Hasekura completely circumvent these problems by approaching Christ from an entirely different angle. The questions of a transcendent God, conscience, sin and the ability or inability to see anything beyond the present world simply do not come up as issues in the faith developments of these three men. Each of them comes to a personal and direct faith in the suffering Christ who remains at their sides through all trials and tribulations. To these Japanese Christians, Christ remains an enigmatic, incomprehensible figure; but perhaps the Son of God, the second person of the Trinity, should remain that way.

---

[128] Endō, *The Samurai*, 406.

[129] Endō very often refers to Christ as *ano hito*, meaning "that person," "that man" or "he" without explicitly using the names "Jesus" or "Christ."

CHAPTER III: THE WAY FORWARD – ENDŌ'S DEVELOPMENT OF A JAPANESE THEOLOGY

In the first phase of his literary career, Endō establishes that the Japanese are different from Europeans. They have a different system of morality and see the world in a different way. The degree of difference is, however, not as great as some would have it and when it comes to behavior and lived experience, there is much overlap. To claim that it is impossible for Japanese to become Christian based on innate anthropological differences is therefore not supportable. Transplanting Christianity is of course difficult, but not impossible.

In the second phase of his literary career, Endō addresses the religious sensibilities of the Japanese. Here, once again, there are indeed differences in how Japanese and Europeans understand God, the cosmos and their place in the universe. To argue, however, that the Japanese are inherently unable to develop a genuine Christian faith or that their faith is always going to be in some way deficient is problematic on two counts. The first is that such a statement assumes that the Westerner has the correct understanding of God, a claim that puts the Westerner at grave danger of hubris. The second is that it seems to say there is only one path to God and one way in which the risen Christ reaches out to people. This carries the danger of reductionism and discounts the variety of ways in which people have come to faith even within the Western tradition.

In the third and final phase of his career, Endō explores alternative ways of encountering Christ that better suit the modern Japanese person. In his 1993 novel, *Deep River*, Endō seems to argue that the difficulty of bringing Christianity into Japan does not have anything to do with any inherent incompatibility between the Christian faith and the Japanese person. There are differences between Japanese and Westerners, but there isn't necessarily anything specific about Japanese people, either from the anthropological perspective or their religious sensibility, that excludes them from Christian faith. The problem is, rather, the Western, European packaging in which Christianity is presented. Through the characters of *Deep River*, Endō lays out the problem with the Eurocentric views associated with Christianity and opens the door for exploring the possibility of a more Japanese theology.

§ 1. DIFFICULTIES FOR JAPANESE PEOPLE

The two main characters of *Deep River*, and the ones in whom most of the questions of theological interest emerge, are the woman Mitsuko and the Japanese Catholic priest Ōtsu. Although Mitsuko flat-out rejects Christianity and Ōtsu commits his life to it, both take issue with the Eurocentrism they see in the Christianity they encounter. Mitsuko is highly suspicious of Christianity, a religion she sees first and foremost as a foreign religion used by European imperial powers as a tool of conquest and control.[130] To her, the European priests and monks are like "weird aliens from another planet," and she resents how they come to Japan to "study" Buddhism and Shinto while retaining their belief that their own religion is superior.[131] She tells Ōtsu that it sets her teeth on edge to think of him, a Japanese person, believing in

---

[130] Endō, *Deep River*, 69.

[131] Endō, *Deep River*, 72, 73.

this European religion.[132] It is almost as if she sees him betraying his country by adopting this foreign faith. Mitsuko's problem with Christianity does not have anything to do with theological or philosophical arguments. For her, the problem is the identification of Christianity with foreignness and European colonialism.

Ōtsu has inherited his Christian faith from his mother and has been Christian his entire life. His Christian faith is deeply embedded within him, and he cannot reject Christianity even when he tries. Having resolved to dedicate his life to Christ and become a priest, he travels to France to enter a seminary in Lyon. When he arrives there, however, he finds himself constantly coming into conflict with his European teachers and fellow seminarians. Like characters in earlier Endō novels, he has difficulty with the dualistic worldview of the Europeans, and cannot easily distinguish between good and evil, light and dark, and black and white. He cannot accept the Western understanding of the cosmos that separates nature from supernature. "I do not believe like you do that God is something external to the human being to be looked up to," he says to his classmates in the seminary, "God is a great life force both within and enveloping human beings, trees, plants and flowers."[133] He has problems with Christianity's claims to absolute truth, and argues that God does not only exist within Christianity, but within Buddhism, Judaism, Hinduism and other religions as well. According to Ōtsu, religious adherence is determined largely by circumstance and not out of any personal choice following scrutinization of various religious traditions. One would

---

[132] Endō, *Deep River*, 105.

[133] Endō, *Deep River*, 191.

expect someone from the Middle East to be Muslim, and someone from India to be Hindu.[134] He says that he "cannot accept that European-style Christianity alone is the absolute truth" and that Christians must dialogue with other religions, but in a way that accepts the genuine validity of the Other's faith, not in the church's inclusivist view that still maintains that Christianity is closer to the ultimate truth than the other religions. He rejects Karl Rahner's idea of "anonymous Christians" as not seeing the other religions on an equal footing with Christianity.[135] Ōtsu's pluralistic views are not welcome with his teachers and classmates at the seminary. For them, "God was raised in our world – the European world you [Ōtsu] hate so much."[136] He is accused of pantheism, told his faith is deficient, denied ordination and expelled from his seminary. He eventually ends up in India, where he helps dying Hindu pilgrims get to the Ganges River.

In these two characters, Endō shows some of the major difficulties Christianity faces when addressing a Japanese audience. Significantly, for both Mitsuko and Ōtsu, the problem does not reside with either Christianity itself or with any inherent aspect of being Japanese, but with the European trappings of Christianity, whether it be the history of colonial aggression or dualistic and exclusivistic worldviews. But is it possible to separate Christianity from European culture and Hellenistic philosophy? Ōtsu certainly hopes so, telling Mitsuko that, "When I eventually get back to Japan... I want to explore a Christianity that fits the hearts of the Japanese."[137]

---

134 Endō, *Deep River*, 196-198.

135 Endō, *Deep River*, 195.

136 Endō, *Deep River*, 311.

What would a "Japanese Christianity" look like? Unfortunately for Ōtsu, the novel ends with him receiving life-threatening injuries before he ever gets the chance to get back to Japan to develop his ideas. By looking at the lives of other characters in the novel, however, one can begin to piece together ideas of what a Japanese theology, and more specifically a Japanese Christology, would focus on.

§ 2. CHRIST THE COMPANION IN SUFFERING

Although Ōtsu is the only Japanese Christian in *Deep River*, several of the other characters have meaningful encounters with Christ-like figures. The first of these is Tsukada, a veteran of the Second World War. Having fought in the disastrous Burma Campaign, he experienced the hellish Japanese retreat along the "Road of Death." Dying of starvation, he committed cannibalism, taking meat from a comrade's corpse. After the war, he is tormented by guilt over his deed, and eventually drinks himself to death. Shortly before dying, however, he finds relief from his guilt by confessing separately to two people: his friend and former comrade, Kiguchi, and the friendly French hospital volunteer, Gaston. As they listen to Tsukada's confession, both Kiguchi and Gaston do their utmost not only to listen, but to join Tsukada in his suffering. Tsukada dies shortly after confessing to Gaston, with a peaceful visage. Kiguchi cannot help but feel that Tsukada died so peacefully because "Gaston took all the pain away from Tsukada's heart."[138] In suffering with Tsukada and loading his pain onto their own shoulders, both Kiguchi and Gaston act as Christ-like figures, like Isaiah's

---

[137] Endō, *Deep River*, 107.

[138] Endō, *Deep River*, 167.

Suffering Servant who "has borne our infirmities and carried our diseases."[139] Gaston also disappears mysteriously at the time of Tsukada's death.

The Suffering Servant of Isaiah 53,2-5 becomes a recurring theme in *Deep River*, and the biblical passage appears in the text several times. Endō even gives chapters 11 and 13 the titles, "Surely he has borne our infirmities and carried our diseases" and "He had no form or majesty that we should look at him," respectively. The Suffering Servant appears later in the form of the Indian goddess Chamunda. Enami, a Japanese tour guide, takes a small group of Japanese tourists into an underground Hindu temple and shows them a statue of Chamunda, a withered, diseased old woman bitten by scorpions and giving milk to the people out of her dried-up breasts. Someone asks him whether Chamunda is like the Indian version of the Virgin Mary. Enami replies, "You could say so, but Chamunda is not pure and refined like the Virgin Mary, and doesn't wear beautiful clothes. Quite the opposite, she is old and ugly, panting with pain, and enduring it. Take a look at her eyes, rolled back and filled with agony. She is suffering together with the Indians."[140] This image of "the one who suffers with" speaks to Enami and reminds him especially of his mother. It also resonates with Kiguchi who remembers all the starving soldiers on the Burmese Road of Death when he looks at Chamunda.

Mitsuko makes the association of Chamunda with the Suffering Servant explicit. Towards the beginning of the novel, Mitsuko picks up a Bible and by chance opens it up to Isaiah 53. When she first reads it, the words are absolutely empty to

---

[139] Is 53,4.

[140] Endō, *Deep River*, 226.

her, and she cannot understand how Ōtsu can find any meaning in them.[141] Her hostility towards Jesus is such that Ōtsu avoids using the name "Jesus" when talking about Christ to her, because he is afraid that the mere mention of the name will put her off.[142] Many years later in India, she reflects on the Chamunda statue and thinks how completely different it is from "the noble, dignified, European Holy Mother." She recalls the words she read from Isaiah 53, and the image of the Suffering Servant overlaps with both Chamunda and Ōtsu. She asks herself, "Why am I searching for 'him'?" and realizes in that moment that she has been chasing after this person who "had no form or majesty" for years without realizing it.[143] Far from being hostile to the Suffering Servant, and perhaps Christ, she now finds herself seeking him.

It seems, then, that Endō supposes that the image of the Suffering Servant would be meaningful for many Japanese people, even if they are not Christian, and, as is the case with Mitsuko, even if they are hostile to Christianity. A Japanese Christology would accordingly place more emphasis on both the suffering of Christ and his steadfast companionship in the suffering of others.

§ 3. CHRIST THE EVER-PRESENT COMPANION AND LISTENER

Closely related to Christ as the companion in suffering is the image of Christ as the loyal and ever-present companion, a theme already present in *The Samurai*. This theme recurs several times in *Deep River*, especially in the life of Ōtsu who at one time abandoned Christ but was never himself

---

[141] Endō, *Deep River*, 71.

[142] Endō, *Deep River*, 200.

[143] Endō, *Deep River*, 286.

abandoned by Christ. To this image of Christ as the loyal companion, Endō adds the image of Christ as the listener through the story of Numata.

Numata is an author of children's books and an animal lover. While he has difficulty confiding in human beings, even his wife, he feels comfortable talking to animals, and sees them as his friends and companions in both sorrow and loneliness. Though not a Christian himself, Numata sees something Christ-like in his pets.[144] "Numata didn't know what God was," explains the narrator, "but if God was the one to whom people can speak from the heart, [the dog] Kuro, the rhinoceros hornbill bird, and the myna bird were God to Numata."[145] This association becomes more explicit in an episode when Numata gets seriously ill. He is hospitalized for a long time, and has only his pet myna bird to talk to. He undergoes a risky operation and barely survives, with doctors later telling him that his heart actually stopped during the surgery. At the same time, the myna bird dies. Upon learning of the bird's death, Numata immediately feels that the bird acted as his substitute (*migawari*) in death.[146]

The point is not that God is in animals, but rather that there was something Christ-like in these animals, and this Christ-like feature was the companionship and the listening ear they gave to Numata. A recurring theme in *Deep River* is of Japanese men who have difficulty expressing themselves to

[144] One of the pets he keeps is a Rhinoceros Hornbill bird he names Pierrot, meaning "clown." Numata is a fan of Georges Rouault, and knows that the artist sometimes represented Christ as a clown. One of these clowns resembles the bird Pierrot (p. 124). This bird becomes his confidant and his sole companion in his loneliness.

[145] Endō, *Deep River*, 130, 131.

[146] Endō, *Deep River*, 133.

anybody, including their wives and children. Numata is one such person, and Isobe, who functions as the archetypical Japanese man, is another.[147] The image of Christ the ever-present companion and listener, the one to whom one can open oneself up completely, would therefore be highly meaningful.

§4. Deus Caritas Est

The final point Endō seems to want to emphasize is the image of God as love. Throughout much of the novel, Mitsuko complains of a profound sense of emptiness within her. Her plight seems to be common, manifesting itself in her university classmates as well. Having no direction in their lives and no movements to inspire them, they try to fill the emptiness with stimulating fun and games. When they enter the working world, their lives revolve around work, golf and cars. Mitsuko knows she is searching for something to fill her void, but she doesn't know what it is. There are indications, however, that what she is searching for is love, as she tries to fill the emptiness with marriage, and when that fails, by doing volunteer work in hospitals, both of which she refers to as actions "imitating love."[148] Unable to find fulfillment in her "imitations of love," she fears that she is unable to truly love anybody, and that not even the sparks of love exist within her.[149] When in India, she watches as Numata takes pity on a group

---

[147] Endō prefaces several of his descriptions of Isobe's inability to communicate with his wife and child with the phrase, "Like most Japanese men, Isobe..." as if to use Isobe as a representative of the ordinary Japanese man. Isobe's wife also refers to him as "Japanese right down to the core," indicating that his behavior is typical of Japanese men of his age.

[148] Endō, *Deep River*, 201.

[149] Endō, *Deep River*, 194.

of lepers. She is annoyed by his "cheap compassion," and the narrator writes that, "She didn't want any more imitations of love. She wanted real love."[150]

The First Letter of St. John contains the famous line proclaimed by Christians everywhere that, "God is love."[151] Before she could even begin digesting this statement, however, Mitsuko would get caught up on the word "God." When Ōtsu tries to describe God to her, she asks him first to stop using the word. "It irritates me and feels meaningless, because it has no real substance to me. Back in college, that word always felt so alien whenever I heard those foreign priests use it."[152] "God" is not only a foreign concept to her, but the word itself is too strongly associated with the foreign priests for her to be able to discuss it in an open way. Ōtsu suggests removing the association with the foreign priests by using a different word for God. They decide to go with "Onion."

Ōtsu tells her several times of his conviction that the Onion is love and that only the Onion can understand her pain and loneliness. At first, she is dismissive and doesn't quite understand what Ōtsu is saying. Gradually, however, she comes to see something meaningful in his words and actions that are motivated by the love between him and the Onion. Ōtsu compares the Onion's love to the Ganges River in the sense that as the Ganges accepts the ashes of all people, the Onion also accepts all, no matter how ugly or dirty they are.[153] Mitsuko does not comprehend what he is saying, but

---

[150] Endō, *Deep River*, 261.

[151] 1 Jn 4,8.

[152] Endō, *Deep River*, 103.

[153] Endō, *Deep River*, 302.

later decides to enter the river to pray. She is skeptical and somewhat embarrassed, saying to herself, "I'm not praying for real, I'm just imitating prayer. Just as I imitated love, I am now imitating prayer." Without realizing it, however, the words sounding in her heart begin to resemble real prayer. "She didn't know to whom she was directing her imitation prayer," the narrator writes. "It may have been to the Onion whom Ōtsu was following. Or it may have been to some great, eternal 'something' that cannot be limited to the term 'Onion'."[154]

Endō makes several significant points in the series of conversations and exchanges between Mitsuko and Ōtsu. The first concerns the "emptiness" that torments not only Mitsuko but her university classmates as well. Endō seems to be saying that the modern generation of Japanese, having achieved amazing economic advancements and no longer suffering from material want, is hungry for some sense of meaning and direction in life. The social discourse that has been going on in Japan since the 1980s would agree with this observation.[155] The second point Endō makes is with regards to the difficulty of using the term "God." In addition to being a difficult word to translate into Japanese,[156] there is also the problem that it is

---

[154] Endō, *Deep River*, 342, 343.

[155] For more on this topic, see the debate surrounding the works of Shintarō Ishihara, especially *"No" to Ieru Nihon* [*The Japan that Can Say "No!"*] (Tokyo: Kōbunsha,1989) and the more recent *Nihonyo* [*Oh, Japan*] (Tokyo: Fusōsha, 2004). In the realm of pop culture, see the works of cartoonist Yoshinori Kobayashi, especially his *Gōmanizumu Sengen* [*Declaration of Arrogance-ism*] series.

[156] The difficulty of finding a term for "God" in Japanese also comes up in *Silence*. The direct translation is *kami*, but there are several problems with this term. First, the Japanese language does not use definite or indefinite

not a neutral word, being too closely associated with the foreign missionaries. This must be taken into account before even beginning a conversation on God, and it may even be useful to use a different name, as Ōtsu does. And finally, he stresses that before speaking about doctrines, one must speak in much more general, amorphous ways about God as love.

In a letter to Mitsuko, Ōtsu describes the difficulties he faced in the five years he spent as a seminarian in France. "The European way of thinking is very clear and logical," he writes. "I couldn't help but admire it, but I couldn't follow it. As an Oriental, I felt that it was too clear and logical, and because of this, it missed something. Their clarity, logic, and way of distinguishing one thing from another were even painful to me."[157] Ōtsu describes a different approach – the approach that led him to seek God:

> In my childhood, of all the things my mother taught me, the only thing I came to believe in was her warmth. The warmth of her hand when she gripped mine, the warmth of her body when she held me. The warmth of love that didn't abandon me, even if I was quite simple-minded compared to my siblings. My mother often spoke to me about the Onion. She taught me that the Onion was a much greater mass of this same warmth. It was, in other words, love itself. I grew up and my mother passed away, but I

articles, so *kami* can mean either "the God" in the monotheistic sense or simply "a god" in the polytheistic sense. Second, Japanese nouns do not change depending on whether they are singular or plural, so *kami* can mean "gods" just as easily as it means "God." Third, the term *kami* in traditional Japanese religion can refer to powerful deities such as the sun goddess Amaterasu Ōmikami, but it can also refer to impersonal spirits of a much lower order, such as river spirits, forest spirits, and the like. Simply translating "God" as "*kami*" can therefore invite misunderstanding.

[157] Endō, *Deep River*, 190.

learned that a piece of the Onion was at the source of my mother's warmth. In the end, the only thing I sought was the Onion's love, and not any of the many doctrines the Church speaks about.[158]

Ōtsu attributes his difficulty with European thinking not to any personal attributes, but to his being Oriental. Endō therefore seems to suggest that speaking about God in terms of logically ordered doctrines would not work with most Japanese people. Much more meaningful would be to speak of God as love in much broader terms rooted in experience.

§ 5. CONCLUSION

In *Deep River*, Endō acknowledges the differences that exist between Japanese and Westerners, but denies that these differences make Christianity meaningless to Japanese. Due to differences in culture and intellectual history, speaking of God in dualistic, logical terms derived from European philosophy will not make the Christian faith accessible to Japanese. There are, however, several other ways to speak of Christ and God, all of which already exist within the Christian tradition, that would resonate with the Japanese person. First, there is the image of Christ as the Suffering Servant who both joins in one's suffering and carries it on his shoulders. Second, there is the Christ as the ever-present companion and listener who alleviates loneliness. And third, there is the understanding of God as the warm, maternal love that both fills and embraces. These images would provide the starting point from which Ōtsu's "Japanese Christianity" could grow.

---

[158] Endō, *Deep River*, 192.

CONCLUSION

> God must be found on the streets of Shinjuku or Shibuya,
> too – districts which seem too far removed from Him… It
> will be one of my tasks to find God in such typical
> Japanese scenes… If I succeed in doing that, my "Western
> suit" will no longer be Western, but will have become my
> own suit. – Shūsaku Endō[159]

In the introduction to the book, *Vitality of East Asian Christianity: Challenges to Mission and Theology in Japan*, Choan Seng Song writes that, "To the world of Christianity Japan is a baffling case."[160] Indeed, it is a baffling case, begging the question, "Why does Christianity not seem to catch on in Japan?" In his novels, *White Man*, *Yellow Man*, *The Sea and Poison*, *Silence*, *The Samurai* and *Deep River*, Shūsaku Endō has attacked this question head-on, providing several possible answers. In the first phase of his career, the discussion was largely anthropological. The Japanese person has no conscience or concept of guilt, is indifferent to death, and cannot distinguish between good and evil. In the second phase of his career, the focus lay more with the religious responses of Japanese people to Christianity. Japanese believers have insufficient or immature faith, they only seek religions with temporal benefits, and they cannot conceive of anything transcendent. At first glance, these seem like rather

[159] Shūsaku Endō as quoted in Mark B. Williams, *Endō Shūsaku: A Literature of Reconciliation*, (London: Routledge, 1999), 33.

[160] Choan Seng Song, introduction to *Vitality of East Asian Christianity: Challenges to Mission and Theology in Japan*, ed. Hidetoshi Watanabe, Keiichi Kaneko and Megumi Yoshida, (Delhi: Indian Society for Promoting Christian Knowledge, 2004), vii.

convincing answers. A more careful reading of his work shows, however, that the actual lived experiences of the characters stand in opposition to all the judgments and assumptions made of Japanese people. Endō doesn't completely negate the differences between Westerners and Japanese, but he does say, "It's not as simple as that."

Choan Seng Song identifies two problems with Christian theology in Japan. The first is that "Christian theology in Japan has often failed to address itself to the problems of the Christian gospel and Japanese culture that many Japanese Christians harbor in their minds, on the one hand, and, on the other, to the issues of life and death people face in their daily lives and in their religious search for the meaning of life." The second problem is that the theology taught in Japan is mostly Western theology. While Western theology isn't bad in and of itself, focusing solely on the West has isolated Japanese theology from the rest of Asia and "delayed the development of theology that can address itself to the social-political and above all religious-cultural world of Japan."[161] In order for Christianity to gain any vitality in Japan, Song argues, Japanese theologians must develop their own theology that speaks to Japanese people.

In the third phase of his career, Endō appears to initiate this. Endō maintains that there are differences between Eastern and Western people, but these do not preclude Japanese from becoming Christians. The problem lies not with Christianity, nor with the Japanese, but with the Western focus of much of Christian theology. Through the characters in *Deep River*, Endō identifies various problems with which today's Japanese people struggle, and begins to explore the

---

[161] Song, x.

possibilities of a Japanese theology that would address these problems.

This essay does not, of course, address all of the theological or human issues in Endō's work. Far more could be written about Endō's Christology and pneumatology, his ideas on pluralism, the demythification of Christianity he seems to support, and so on. What I hope to have demonstrated in this paper is that, first, far from arguing that it is impossible for Japanese to become Christians, as a first reading of his work might suggest, Endō says that, "No, it is possible for Japanese to become Christians;" and, second, that Endō gives us a glimpse of what a Japanese Christianity would begin to look like.

As a final thought, Endō's work is not relevant only for Japan. Many of the complaints his characters raise against the Church are also brought up by people in the West. Many of the difficulties his characters experience in life are also prevalent in Europe, North America, and possibly many other parts of the world. After all, many of the problems Endō's characters grapple with are human problems as well as Japanese problems. As the Church continues to seek new ways to keep Christianity relevant for each successive generation of people, perhaps an alternative perspective – the "yellow" perspective – would help.

WORKS CITED

Barrett, David B., George Thomas Kurian, and Todd M. Johnson. *World Christian Encyclopedia: A Comparative Survey of Churches and Religions in the Modern World.* 2nd ed. New York: Oxford University Press, 2001.

Benedict, Ruth. *The Chrysanthemum and the Sword: Patterns of Japanese Culture.* New Edition. London: Routledge & Kegan Paul Limited, 1977.

Endō, Shūsaku. *Chinmoku [Silence].* Tokyo: Shinchōsha, 1966; reprint 2007.

—. *Fukai Kawa [Deep River].* Tokyo: Shinchōsha, 1993; reprint 2009.

—. *Samurai [The Samurai].* Tokyo: Shinchōsha, 1980; reprint 2009.

—. *Shiroi Hito Kiiroi Hito [White Man, Yellow Man].* Tokyo: Shinchōsha, 1955; reprint 2010.

—. *Umi to Dokuyaku [The Sea and Poison].* Tokyo: Shinchōsha, 1958; reprint 2010.

Kisala, Robert. "Japanese Religions." In *Nanzan Guide to Japanese Religions*, edited by Paul L. Swanson and Clark Chilson, 3-13. Honolulu: University of Hawai'i Press, 2006.

Kumazawa, Yoshinobu. Foreword to *Christianity in Japan, 1971 - 1990*, edited by Yoshinobu Kumazawa and David L. Swain, xiii - xvi. Tokyo: Kyo Bun Kwan (The Christian Literature Society of Japan), 1991.

Mase-Hasegawa, Emi. *Christ in Japanese Culture: Theological Themes in Shusaku Endo's Literary Works.* Leiden: Brill, 2008.

Miyazaki, Kentarō. "Roman Catholic Mission in Pre-Modern Japan." in *Handbook of Christianity in Japan (Handbook of Oriental Studies – Part 5: Japan, 10),* edited by Mark R. Mullins, 1-18. Leiden: Brill Academic Publishing, 2003.

Mullins, Mark R. "Japanese Christianity." In *Nanzan Guide to Japanese Religions,* edited by Paul L. Swanson and Clark Chilson, 115-128. Honolulu, HI: University of Hawai'i Press, 2006.

Saeki, Shōichi. Commentary to *Umi to Dokuyaku [The Sea and Poison],* by Shūsaku Endō, 197-208. Tokyo: Shinchōsha, 1958; reprint 2010.

Second Vatican Council. "Gaudium et Spes." December 7, 1965. http://www.vatican.va/archive/hist_councils/ii_vatica n_council/documents/vat-ii_cons_19651207_gaudium-et-spes_en.html (accessed May 12, 2011).

Shimazono, Susumu. "New Religious Movements." In *Religion & Society in Modern Japan,* edited by Mark R. Mullins, Susumu Shimazono and Paul L. Swanson, 221-230. Berkeley: Asian Humanities Press, 1993.

Song, Choan Seng. Introduction to *Vitality of East Asian Christianity: Challenges to Mission and Theology in Japan,* edited by Hidetoshi Watanabe, Keiichi Kaneko and Megumi Yoshida, vii-xi. Delhi: Indian Society for Promoting Christian Knowledge, 2004.

Swyngedouw, Jan. "Religion in Contemporary Japanese Society." In *Religion & Society in Modern Japan,* edited by Mark R. Mullins, Susumu Shimazono and Paul L. Swanson, 49-72. Berkeley: Asian Humanities Press, 1993.

Williams, Mark B. *Endō Shūsaku: A Literature of Reconciliation.* London: Routledge, 1999.

Printed by Amazon Italia Logistica S.r.l.
Torrazza Piemonte (TO), Italy

53049159R00050